BUSHIDO
AND THE ART OF LIVING

An Inquiry into Samurai Values

ALEXANDER BENNETT

JAPAN PUBLISHING INDUSTRY FOUNDATION FOR CULTURE

Bushido and the Art of Living: An Inquiry into Samurai Values
Alexander Bennett

First published 2017
by Japan Publishing Industry Foundation for Culture (JPIC)
3-12-3 Kanda-Jinbocho, Chiyoda-ku, Tokyo 101-0051, Japan

Paperback edition: 2019

©2013 by Alexander Bennett
English translation © 2017 by Japan Publishing Industry Foundation for Culture
All rights reserved

Originally published in Japanese under the title of *Nihonjin no shiranai bushido* by Bungeishunju Ltd. in 2013.

English-language edition published with permission from Bungeishunju Ltd.

Book design by Jennifer Piatkowski

Printed in Japan
ISBN 978-4-86658-051-7
http://www.jpic.or.jp/japanlibrary/

JAPAN LIBRARY

CONTENTS

Preface 5

Introduction: Ever-Changing Bushido 17

1. *Zanshin*: Lingering Mind and the Essence of Bushido 33

2. *Koyo-gunkan* and the Ideal Leader 75

3. Dead Ready to Live: *Hagakure* and *Budo-shoshinshu* 103

4. Live and Let Live: The Life-Giving Sword 149

5. Bushido: The Dark and the Light 177

Afterword 219

Bibliography 223

About the Author 227

Preface

This is a translation of a book I wrote in Japanese in 2013 titled *Nihonjin no Shiranai Bushido* (The Bushido that Japanese don't know). It is not meant to be a scholarly discourse on the concept of Bushido—the Way of the samurai warrior—which, for various reasons, modern Japanese pride themselves on as a momentous component of their moral fabric. Although my academic career has mostly been spent investigating the role that Bushido and the martial arts (budo) play in the formulation of a Japanese sense of national identity, this book is more a collection of personal thoughts and ponderings pertaining to the substance and relevance of samurai culture today, from over three decades of justifying my own obsession with waving sticks around in the dojo.

I question the commonly held notion that Bushido is imbued in the DNA of Japanese people by virtue of being born in Japan, and unquestioned acclamations of Bushido as something that is inherently good. That is not to say that I think the fifty shades of Bushido should be discarded as a fanciful, romantic load of rubbish that is potentially dangerous and absurdly outdated. Far from it. There is a wellspring of universal wisdom in "them thar Japanese hills," and if you know what you are looking for, it is truly profound.

The sundry books that expound the virtues of Bushido as something that must be preserved or revived for Japan to maintain its national power, however, are typical of extreme nationalist proponents. "We Japanese have Bushido flowing through our veins; *post hoc ergo propter hoc*, we are unique, noble and awesome. But young Japanese in their decadence are spoiling the party. Praise be to the samurai spirit. Let us become born-again *bushi*—righteous, courageous, benevolent, polite, sincere, honorable, and loyal. …Let's make Japan great again."

One look at my pink face and blue eyes should be enough to convince most that I am no ultranationalist Japanese. And, in case you are wondering, although I love Japan and its people and culture, I do not consider myself to be a one-eyed apologist either. Having lived in Japan for nearly three decades now—much longer than in my birth country, New Zealand—I am often viewed by Japanese people as "more Japanese than the Japanese." I take issue with this. I just see myself as Alex Bennett, someone who embraces many, sometimes conflicting Japanese and Kiwi cultural traits. Let me just say, I like to revel in the best of both worlds.

I see all sorts of non-Japanese come and go in Japan, including those I call "Geekus Nipponica." They have an infuriating enthusiasm for everything Japanese, irrespective of whether it is good or bad. If it is Japanese, "then it's gotta be *kakko ii* (cool)" type of kid-in-a-candy-shop mentality that barely scratches the surface of reality. They also have uncanny but stilted knowledge about Japanese culture and history gleaned through manga and videogames. Geekus Nipponica are inevitably popular with the locals because of their naive but unbridled enthusiasm for Japan.

Then, there are the "Japandroids." They discard their true identities at Narita Airport and do everything in their power to dress, act, and speak like a Japanese. It is the Japandroid who hankers to be called "more Japanese than the Japanese," and they smugly soak up the attention, believing that this is the ultimate homage and acceptance of his/her successful assimilation. I know this because they are phases that I also went through. Rather than "assimilating," however, I think I have successfully "integrated" myself into the Japanese way of life and see myself as having evolved into a "Zenling"—someone who is comfortable in his own skin.

Like everywhere else, Japan has its wonderful features counterbalanced by idiosyncrasies that are quite irksome. One thing that I find particularly vexatious is the one-dimensional public extolling of Bushido. It is in my nature as a scholar to be skeptical. I am usually suspicious of the way Bushido is superficially bandied about in Japan (and in the West, for that matter) as the be-all and end-all to the human condition. But, then, you may well ask, "Isn't that what this book is about?" Yes, it is an affirmation of Bushido as a relevant source of wisdom for those living in the twenty-first century, Japanese or otherwise; but my approach is very different from that of the standard eulogies for Bushido. Let me explain why.

The word "Bushido" became known throughout the world largely thanks to Nitobe Inazo's classic *Bushido: The Soul of Japan* (1899). This book was written in English and intended for an audience outside Japan. He discussed the morals and customs of Japanese society and its Confucian, Buddhist, and Shinto influences vis-à-vis the religion and philosophies of the West. Educated in Japan in English, Nitobe was an expert in agriculture and colonial administration, not Japanese history or thought. The degree to which the content of his book represents "true" Bushido, whatever that is, is questionable.

One thing about Bushido that so many commentators fail to factor into their evaluation is how its nature has changed greatly over time from the Warring States period (1467–1568) through the Edo period (1603–1868), again in the Meiji period (1868–1912); then, there is the post-samurai era of reinvented modern Bushido of prewar Japan, postwar Japan, right up to the present day. My first order of business, then, is to stress that no single definition of Bushido covers all uses of the term, but I employ it for convenience. Actually, the word "Bushido" did not become widely used until the late Meiji period, after the samurai class had disappeared. While some scholars may wish to argue this point, other appellations such as *shido* (way of the gentleman) or *budo* (the martial way; not to be confused with modern martial arts) were more representative of the warrior ethos in the Edo period, for example, and many more designations were used before this. Now, of course, Bushido is the ubiquitous term denoting the samurai code of honor irrespective of the era, and the vast majority's understanding today is premised on Nitobe's interpretation.

When I first wrote this book in Japanese, my question to readers was: How many people truly understand the meaning of the word? It is a rhetorical question, and a cheeky one at that, especially coming from somebody not born with Bushido DNA. I am not Japanese. I come from New Zealand. I first arrived in Japan to study Japanese when I was seventeen in 1987—the height of the bubble economy. My motivation was purely economic. If I could master the Japanese language, I thought, then I was guaranteed a piece of the Japanese pie.

Mastering Japanese cultural pursuits was not on my radar at all. I fell into kendo purely by accident, but, looking back, stepping foot in that high school dojo in January 1987 was the most fateful moment of my life. One training session, in particular, did turn me into a kind of "born-again *bushi*." It sounds like a teenage Japandroid fantasy, but it was not exactly pleasant or something I wished for. It was the most mind-blowingly frightening ordeal imaginable for a beleaguered young foreigner trying to navigate Wonderland. I felt like a pile of dust on the floor, ready to blow away with a gust of wind. More on this trial by fire later.

Suffice it to say, it was a turning point for me—the juncture at which I started my perpetual journey trying to make sense of the Way of the warrior. For nearly thirty years now, I have devoted myself to the practice of kendo and other martial arts. I am currently ranked seventh level (*dan*) in kendo, and in other martial arts, fifth *dan* in *naginata*, *iaido*, *jukendo*, and *tankendo*. I have also spent many years studying the classical martial arts of Kashima Shinden Jikishin Kage-ryu swordsmanship, the Tendo-ryu tradition of *naginata-jutsu*, and the Hoki-ryu tradition of *iaijutsu*. Not a day goes by that I do not pick up some kind of weapon in the dojo and transmute into a maniacal sword-wielding demon.

My initial aspiration to become a well-heeled bilingual international lawyer made way for the misty world of Bushido research. My study of martial arts and Bushido has been an inquiry into the nature of the samurai mind and ethics, and there is no end in sight. What have I gained from this experience? What compels me to keep going? What is the point of budo anyway? And how is it related to the ambiguous ramblings on Bushido that pop up here and there in Japan? These are some of the questions I address in this book.

In the past few years, people have been re-examining the nature of Bushido anew. One might even call it a "boom," but there have been many in the past, and there will no doubt be many more in the future, reflecting fluctuations in the political and social climate. Books on the subject continue to adorn shelves in bookshops, and the lion's share dwell on the idea that, in Japan at present, morals are declining, politics and the economy are rudderless, and men are becoming weak and effeminate. The traditional warrior spirit is put forward as sadly lacking. Most of these discussions are personal interpretations of the writings of the samurai of the past, and force abstract conclusions along the lines of "Bushido is the source of the spirit of the Japanese people. Thank you, Dr. Nitobe."

For example, in 2005 *Kokka no hinkaku* (Dignity of the Nation) became a runaway best-seller. The author, a mathematics professor named Fujiwara Masahiko, outlined myriad social problems plaguing Japan. "People need to develop aesthetic sensitivity and revive Japanese emotions. Japanese need a certain schematic for their spirit." Bushido, he suggested, is the solution. The author has little to say about how, specifically, Japan might revive this "warrior spirit." There is an all too common tendency to slap a coat of Bushido over everything to seal the cracks, but this is little more than building castles in the sky.

Based on my own experiences, I believe that the practice of budo provides tangible clues as to how this castle can be built on terra firma instead. The biggest hole in postwar acclamations of Bushido, in my opinion, is that they are divorced from actual practice in the martial arts. Mastery of the military arts and the evolution of the warrior ethos in Japan were concomitant. You cannot have one without the other.

Bizarrely, not many recent Bushido propagandists have made this connection. Few martial artists care to study the history or literature of the samurai, and few historians or literary experts care to study martial arts. So, all have missed the bleedingly obvious connection or at best have only made perfunctory associations between budo and Bushido.

It is about walking the talk. Bushido will never be truly appreciated solely through deskbound discussions. Lofty ideals might look good on paper but must also be understood with the body, not just intellect; this comes only through practice and experience. My consistent message for some time now in Japan has been that a "revival of budo" is far more palpable than a "revival of Bushido." Reading old samurai tactical manuals and treatises on life backed up with thousands of hours in the dojo makes the content much more interesting and germane. It all starts to make sense. After thirty years of kendo training, for example, I have gradually come to "get" what legendary warriors such as Yagyu Munenori or Miyamoto Musashi wrote in their timeless classics. You feel it in the core of the gut, but the gut needs to be strengthened through hard training first.

Of course, studying martial arts alone is not enough to draw water from the well of Bushido knowledge. I think of it as two wheels of a cart. Through physical participation in budo, one can access the philosophical tenets of Bushido, which essentially provides the underlying ideology for modern martial disciplines. At least, those immersed in the study of budo will have a better chance of comprehending various aspects of Bushido and the warrior ethos than those who have not.

Someone like me, a non-Japanese, is naturally going to have a different take on things such as Bushido and budo. People often tell me that Bushido is a spiritual culture unique to Japan, but I do not share this view. I believe that Bushido has important lessons for all of us because it conveys values that are unchanging, transcending time and place. Perhaps this is clearer to me because I am not Japanese, and I have continually had to justify to myself why I should continue living in Japan to reconnoitre samurai culture. Having a totally different perspective helps one read between the lines in the most unlikely ways. Thus, my experience as a non-Japanese adherent of budo in Japan is not as disadvantageous as it might seem.

Now, on with the story. In the Introduction to this book I give a brief overview of the history of Bushido in which I introduce the main themes of the book. In Chapter 1, I discuss the concept of *zanshin* (lingering mind = physical and psychological vigilance). This is an important term used in martial arts to denote the state of not relaxing one's guard after an attack. It also incorporates both respect and compassion for one's opponent/enemy. To me, *zanshin* is the essence of martial arts. It can be applied to many aspects of everyday life.

In Chapter 2, I examine a Bushido classic, *Koyo-gunkan*, which tells the tales of Takeda Shingen and other luminous warriors of the Warring States period. It sheds light on how those who lead organizations, warlords in this case, should conduct themselves and is replete with apt lessons for the management and administration of institutions in modern times.

In Chapter 3, I focus on two more important but terribly misunderstood early-modern books: *Hagakure* and *Budo-shoshinshu*. They are representative of the Edo-period accounts of Bushido, through which we can learn how the samurai lived in constant awareness of their impending death. This "awareness" of or "contempt" for death is the core consideration of Bushido and is what makes it such a fascinating canon of beliefs and behavior.

Chapter 4 is a discussion of peace and the renunciation of war based on another Edo-period Bushido masterpiece, *Heiho-kadensho*. It demonstrates how the techniques for killing must ultimately transform into techniques for living. These are but a tiny selection of hundreds of other books that I could introduce to illustrate these points and examine the true depth and complexity of Bushido in terms of the dichotomies it reflects: life and death, strength and kindness, the loyalty and independence. I chose them because they are readily available in bookshops today, even in English.

Finally, Chapter 5 is a look back over my life in Japan so far and my involvement with budo. What are the possibilities for budo going forward? What are some of the serious problems that budo faces as it struggles to maintain its traditions while remaining relevant in the twenty-first century?

The origins of Bushido are in the medieval battlefields of Japan, where samurai never knew whether they would live to see another day. Questions of life and death and of how to live life to its full potential are not unique to the samurai experience. We all face these issues. The wisdom of the samurai, however, is poignant in that it was premised on an acceptance of the ethereality of human existence. They recorded it meticulously for us in their literature and in the martial arts, which have evolved over time as a lasting vestige of samurai culture. This is precisely why Bushido fascinates people all over the world. Like the modern budo sports, it extends beyond national borders and beyond categories of race or religion.

Such are the high expectations the government has for budo education, it was made a compulsory subject in physical education classes for middle-school pupils in Japan from 2012. This is something that I, as a regular practitioner, should welcome, given what I have just written about "reviving budo." Nevertheless, we must also remain ever-mindful of the potential dangers of budo. The martial arts and Bushido were created in conflict, and the techniques are potentially lethal. Budo is not ping pong. Without this element of danger, the experience and lessons become significantly diluted. The problem is where to draw the line.

The inclusion of karate in the 2020 Tokyo Olympics makes this an opportune time to discuss the immense possibilities of the martial arts, including the potential for danger. With the eyes of the world taking notice of the judo and karate competitions in 2020, Japanese martial arts will have more international exposure than ever before. I hope that this book in some way contributes to a deeper understanding of the psychological underpinnings of the incredible culture of budo.

Note on Translation

In general, Japanese names that appear in this book are given in Japanese order, with the surname first.

I would like to express my heartfelt gratitude to Peter MacMillan and his wonderful staff who oversaw production of the English-language version. Thanks also to Terry Gallagher, Okamoto Hirotsugu, Ikenobe Tomoko, Kataoka Yoshihiro, Media Press, and Bungei Shunju.

To my *naginata* teacher, Kimura Yasuko.

INTRODUCTION

Ever-Changing Bushido

Overview of the Samurai Way

Let me begin with an introduction of this rather vague term, "Bushido"—the Way of the warrior. Although its meaning has been in constant flux with each passing era in Japan, broadly speaking, it can be divided into three categories:

1. The pragmatic ethos of the samurai before the Edo period (1603–1868)—a philosophy forged out of the experiences of war. (The term Bushido did not exist then.)

2. The Bushido promoted by the Confucian and military scholars of the Edo period. The Edo period was an extended epoch of peace throughout Japan, and the warrior ethos was tweaked to promote the maintenance of social order.

3. The intellectual Bushido of the Meiji period (1868–1912) and beyond. This represents a reinterpretation of samurai culture in the post-samurai world in the formulation of a modern national identity for the Japanese people as a whole.

Who were the samurai? In a nutshell, they were specialist warriors who developed their own subculture placing "honor" and the avoidance of "shame" above all else. They became a significant political force in Japan with the initiation of the Kamakura period (1185–1333)—so named after the warrior government that was established in the little town of Kamakura not far from present-day Tokyo. The warrior capital was geographically removed from the aristocratic government located in Kyoto, and although the samurai elite in Kamakura and nobles of the imperial court shared a common ancestry and were on level footing politically, a very different culture emerged from their life in the hinterlands. The ethos of the Kamakura period warrior was premised on loyalty underlined by a fierce spirit of autonomy. The idioms of honor in the samurai community revolved around their ability to fight and prevail in the violence that permeated their way of life. Happy to sacrifice their lives as expressions of fealty to their lords—or so the old war tales inform us—they were hard, rustic men who revelled in the rough-and-ready lifestyle of the frontier.

Samurai culture became increasingly sophisticated during the Muromachi period (1333–1573), when the warrior government was reestablished in the Muromachi section of Kyoto. Although an honorable reputation gleaned through combat prowess remained at the heart of the warrior, it became tempered by a new appreciation for the arts and a burgeoning sense of aestheticism that was as urbane as the court protocols after which it was modelled. As the influence of the aristocracy declined, the samurai were well equipped militarily and culturally to take the reins of power once and for all.

Crucial to this new samurai ethos was the notion of *bunbu-ryodo*—cultivating a balance of competency in cultural and military arts, or "brush and sword in accord." The samurai of this time were devoted to honing their martial abilities as the craft of war demanded, but they had also become fixated on questions of morality, cultivation of the self, fostering aesthetic sensibilities, and spirituality.

Books such as *Chikubasho* (Bamboo Stilt Anthology, 1383) demonstrate this transition. A treatise on warrior deportment written for the edification of young men of his clan by Shiba Yoshimasa (1350–1410), it declares that warriors and religious adherents share a common kind of ascetic spirituality: "A man whose profession is arms should be serene in mind, and able to see deeply into the hearts of others." Yoshimasa combines Buddhist concepts of compassion and "killing one's own ego" with Confucian morals of loyalty and filial piety as requisite factors in a warrior's manner. He also talks of the need for heightened awareness in the pursuit of artistic perfection. This was to develop character and enhance the reputation of the clan. "Above all, a samurai must act in the interests of his own honor, as well as the honor of his descendants. Life is regrettably short, but one's reputation must remain unstained for eternity."

What kind of act would stain a warrior's honor? "Dying profligately before one's time by treating precious life as no more than dust and ashes would bring about unspeakable repute." Living a precarious existence in a turbulent time, samurai refined their own characteristic modus operandi for existing in style on a knife's edge. The samurai embraced the eternal beauty of impermanence, for nobody gets out of life alive—a truism they faced every minute of the day. The quest, then, was to find the right cause to die for when the time came.

Values Born of Battle

The Onin War (1467) brought about an inversion in Japanese society. Regional warlords vied for power over the ensuing century and a half in what is known as the Sengoku (Warring States) period (1467–1603). As the era name suggests, it was a time of civil war and treachery, in which, to use a popular Japanese aphorism, "the strong eat, and the weak are meat." In other words, military might and strategic guile were the key to survival and supremacy. What tenets of pragmatic knowledge guided samurai so that they could take a seat at the dinner table, as opposed to becoming dinner?

Clues can be found in *Koyo-gunkan*—a fascinating book that offers a window into the minds of Sengoku warriors. It relates the personal philosophy of Takeda Shingen, one of Japan's most redoubtable warlords, and is a vivid account of the way the samurai lived through the turmoil. The late Sagara Toru, preeminent scholar of Japanese history and thought, wrote that *Koyo-gunkan* is a "chronicle of moral values that shaped the Warring States period." Terms such as *bu-no-michi* (martial way), *otoko-no-michi* (manly way), and *yumiya toru mi no narai* (customs of those who live by the bow and arrow) were some of the many used to designate warrior ideals. It was in the *Koyo-gunkan*, a collection of miscellaneous notes on military affairs, that we first come across the word "Bushido." *Koyo-gunkan* is redolent with hard nosed wisdom borne of actual combat. Therefore, it came to hold considerable sway among samurai during the peaceful Edo period as they ruminated on the warrior's Way.

Numerous treatises written in medieval Japan uphold the imperative for absolute allegiance to one's lord. If anything, this is an indication of the variability of hierarchical relationships at the time. Shingen established the "Koshu hatto no shidai" (Koshu Laws) to govern his provinces, setting forth a moral and legal code for his men to obey. Much of the content was premised on the idea that the bond between vassal and master must be akin to that of parent and child. Perusing the leaves of *Koyo-gunkan*, one becomes acutely aware of the responsibility of the leader to be worthy of loyal apostles, and the dilemma that a samurai faced when his loyalty and sense of individuality clashed. This tension in self-awareness, between the group and the individual, presents one of the thorniest contradictions in the life of the samurai throughout their long history.

Samurai were obliged to obey the laws of their province or face punishment by death; but, as proud warriors for whom heroism was a calling card, they might also be obligated to break the law if it meant the preservation of personal honor. The samurai's potent sense of principle dictated that he be honest with himself, even if it meant contravening his lord's decrees; not to do so would mean he was weak, cared little for his reputation, and was therefore not worthy of his status.

Such existential propositions became increasingly burdensome during the Edo period, which is why *Koyo-gunkan* became required reading for future generations as they tried to grapple with their heritage as warriors in a time of peace. As much as it is a useful study of Takeda clan military strategy, it is also a perceptive account of human nature and an exposé on what constitutes purity in action and thought from the samurai perspective.

The Impact of Confucianism in the Edo Period

As the curtain came down on the tempestuous Sengoku period, the way of the warrior underwent a process of reconstruction to realign the volatile samurai mind-set with an unfamiliar world of peace. A change to more placid times required a kind of mentality and behavior different from the honor-fuelled violent free-for-alls of yesteryear.

A new social order was fashioned that placed samurai at the top of the ladder, followed by farmers, artisans, and merchants. The classes had a degree of fluidity, and the distinction between them was not as clear cut as often portrayed. Still, the samurai were officially at the apex of the pecking order and expected to conduct themselves as worthy leaders of society.

The Edo period warrior ethos was multifarious but generally summarized as having been based on certain crucial elements: Confucian ideals of social order, individualistic avowals of "undying" fealty to one's overlord and domain, a Buddhist appreciation of the ephemeral world, and a spiritual outlook on death. These fundamentals can be described as representing the soft and hard sides of the Edo period warrior ethos. With the onset of peace, prominent Confucian and military scholars set about clarifying and justifying the role and position of warriors. The term *shido* (Way of the gentleman) was coined to describe consummate warrior deportment in a warless world.

In the words of Kanno Kakumyo, *shido* was essentially the philosophy that refocused the samurai psyche in accordance with Confucian mores. In the early years of the Edo period, scholars such as Nakae Toju (1607–48), for example, advanced a formula for the warrior's way based on the teachings of Zhu Xi (1130–1200), and then on Wang Yangming's (1472–1529) philosophy. He taught the validity of fostering morality through conscience-based action. This concept dictated that samurai aspire to live virtuous lives in accordance with the paradigms of humanity and justice, perform duties diligently, as their station required, and dedicate themselves to maintaining peace in the realm.

In Nakae Toju's treatise "Dialogue on Cultural and Military Arts," the former consisted of genteel pursuits, such as literature and poetry, while "military" referred to archery, swordsmanship, horsemanship, tactics, and so on. In essence, the two realms were interlocking aspects of one whole. Cultural and military arts were a duality like heaven and earth or yin and yang. Literary skill, for example, without commensurate ability in military affairs was flawed and incomplete.

Yamaga Soko (1622–85) was another prominent neo-Confucian military scholar who maintained that samurai *ipseity* came from self-cultivation through mastery of cultural and military arts. In his influential writings and lectures, Soko reasoned that every aspect of daily life was an opportunity for polishing the self and admonished samurai to behave as paragons of morality to the masses. After all, samurai did not make or grow anything, so they had to be useful in other ways. Why not be role models and show the other classes what dedication to duty was all about?

Soko and his disciples believed in a practical way of life. The true determinant of a samurai's worth, they argued, was not honor on the battlefield (as there was no longer any to be had); rather, it was in how he conducted himself in the mundane affairs of daily life. The root of their argument was still premised on an "awareness of death," but in a much more conceptual way than the warrior ethos of the Sengoku period.

Japanese DNA?

Following the Meiji Restoration of 1868, "samurai" status and the various privileges that came with it were dismantled, and all Japanese were theoretically made equal under the law. One might think that, with the dissolution of samurai as a class, Bushido would also disappear into the ether, but this proved to be far from the case. On the contrary, a new interpretation of Bushido emerged that served as a powerful emotive force in the process of modernization and the creation of a national identity.

Japan began to draft young men into the military in 1873. All men over the age of twenty, unless they had the wherewithal to buy their way out, were required to undergo military training. Until this time, military affairs had principally been the domain of samurai. In this sense, the "Conscription Edict" signalled a revolutionary social change.

With the promulgation of the "Imperial Rescript to Soldiers and Sailors" in 1882, all young men, irrespective of their family lineage, were indoctrinated in a modern military code of honor. The document does not mention the word "Bushido" per se, but its description of the "ideal soldier" makes ample reference to quintessential samurai values, such as "loyalty," "propriety," and "frugality"—all keywords in the works of Yamaga Soko and countless other writings on Bushido during the Edo period and before. Near the end of the "Imperial

Rescript to Soldiers and Sailors" for example, is a passage that reads: "Know that death is lighter than a goose feather." It is a quote from the late-eleventh-century war tale *Mutsu waki*. Although samurai existed no more as a social entity, their moral legacy was being mixed into the foundation concrete for modern Japanese identity.

"The Imperial Rescript to Soldiers and Sailors" was distributed to and memorized by all soldiers and sailors as their official code of ethics. It encouraged absolute loyalty to the emperor, as a samurai was to his lord, and honorable deportment in selfless service of the nation, as a samurai did for his domain. The "Rescript" remained the cornerstone of imperial armed forces comportment as Japan headed down the slippery slope of militarism, until it crashed on the other side in 1945. The young men in Japan's military were taught to consider themselves modern incarnations of samurai, embodying the same never-say-die-until-death martial spirit.

Another document, "The Imperial Rescript on Education" (1890), also played its part in spurring citizens to worship the emperor and contribute selflessly to the future prosperity of Japan. Memorized by all schoolchildren, its content accentuates Japan's uniqueness in the world and implores loyal subjects to "advance public good and promote common interests" and should emergency arise, "offer yourselves courageously to the state."

Like many countries in the late nineteenth century, Japan was awash with burgeoning nationalism and engaged in a quest for collective distinctiveness. It was a time when Japanese were becoming keenly aware of their common identity as an inimitable people in terms of history, traditions, and customs vis-à-vis the rest of the world, and documents such as "The Imperial Rescript on Education" beseeched Japanese youth to "render illustrious the best traditions of your forefathers." What tradition was more worthy of rendering illustrious than the noble way of the samurai?

Bushido was reinterpreted and disseminated as the spiritual pulse of the nation. Victory in the First Sino-Japanese War (1894–95) marked the start of a new, more pugnacious Japan and stimulated a revival of popular interest in samurai traditions. Then, riding a wave of confidence and aspirations to expand the empire, Japan pulled off the unthinkable. To the astonishment of the West, Japan emerged victorious in the Russo-Japanese War of 1904–5. The world was besotted by the Japanese strength of character, discipline, and hardiness that enabled this feat. What, many pundits pondered, made Japan tick? More to the point, what lessons could Westerners learn from such enigmatic Japanese savvy to better serve their own countries?

Late in the Meiji period, Inoue Tetsujiro, a Tokyo Imperial University professor of philosophy, summed up the exploit in his usual jingoistic tone. "Japan engaged a fearsome opponent and summarily defeated it in a short-lived fight. This was a truly outstanding victory, more conclusive than David's trouncing of Goliath. The people of other nations are in awe of Japan." Little more than thirty years had passed since the Meiji Restoration ushered Japan out of the feudal era. How, in such a short time span, had Japan secured a reputation as a modern military force to be reckoned with? Westerners and Japanese alike excitedly dissected the secrets to Japan's stupendous success and often came to the same conclusion: "It must be thanks to Bushido, of course." The Japanese people had been "samuraified," and the spirit of Bushido "flowed through their veins." Following lauded military successes in China and then over Russia, Japan was becoming increasingly partial to the sweet nectar of Bushido.

As luck would have it for the Japanese polymath and Christian Nitobe Inazo, his book *Bushido: The Soul of Japan* (1899), which he penned in English, became an instant best-seller. It remains popular and is the most-quoted book on Bushido to this day. The Japanese version, titled simply *Bushido*, was translated from English in 1908 and subsequently became fashionable in Japan thanks to the rave reviews it was receiving everywhere else. It was Nitobe's view that Bushido was the "moral backbone" of the Japanese.

Although Inoue Tetsujiro was a harsh critic of Nitobe's interpretation, he also proclaimed that Bushido was "the spiritual framework that makes the Japanese people Japanese." In the age when samurai did exist, they constituted no more than five percent or six percent of the population. It is curious that the customs of a small group of social elites could blossom into the spirit of the nation, to the extent that Bushido is amorously claimed to be enmeshed in the genetic fabric of the Japanese even now.

To quote Inoue again, "It was nothing other than Bushido that elevated Japan to its rightful place on the world stage. Bushido is a spiritual culture in its own right, and being the indigenous ethical code of Japan, it is precisely what makes the Japanese people sui generis." To a liberal-minded cynic, this conclusion may seem irrational and preposterous. Nevertheless, illustrious scholars, reporters, politicians, authors, musicians, xenophobes—in fact, the gamut of people in Japan have been passively (on occasion, forcibly) indoctrinated into this way of thinking over the past 120 years and seldom bother to deconstruct the notion to see whether it holds any water. It has become a truism.

Good and Bad Bushido

In the late Meiji period, myriad books were published on the subject of Bushido, and more than a few were inspired by Nitobe's seminal work. Ironically, the word "Bushido" was not particularly common until it became a moniker of Japan's process of modernization. In this sense, the tenor of Bushido that most people know today is very much an invented tradition.

Such an invention of terms, or, shall we just say, the "wistful revival" of glorious traditions from the past, was by no means peculiar to the Japanese experience. In *The Invention of Tradition*, British scholar Eric Hobsbawm writes, "Traditions which appear or claim to be old are often quite recent in origin and sometimes invented." Furthermore, "They are highly relevant to that comparatively recent historical innovation, the 'nation,' with its associated phenomena: nationalism, the nation-state, national symbols, histories and the rest." Any historian will tell you that all traditions are invented, so this is no great revelation. However, the thought that prevalent contemporary perceptions of Bushido may also be a modern creation of the samurai-less age is virtually unheard-of in Japan.

Nitobe emphasized shared values in Western and Japanese morality. His intention was to whet the appetite of Westerners who hungered to know more about the rapid modernization of Japan, its culture, and its people. To this end, he declares that the ethical beliefs of Bushido were passed from samurai to commoners through the medium of popular culture and became the moral mainstay of modern Japanese through osmosis.

For example, propriety, righteousness, compassion, honor, and self-discipline were identified by Nitobe as traditional Japanese virtues emanating from the warrior canon. It would be more correct to say, however, that these were unassailable moral values that Nitobe himself embraced, rather than anything directly related to Bushido. Although born into a samurai family, a curious but little known fact is that Nitobe's actual understanding of Bushido was questionable, to the point that he even admitted to originally believing the word was his own creation, and he was surprised to find that it already existed.

Inoue Tetsujiro and others more qualified to lecture on the history of samurai ethics criticized Nitobe's work sharply. The most common complaint was that he had "Christianized" samurai ideals, rather than representing them in their true form. Nitobe was Christian—a Quaker to be precise—and there is some truth to this assertion. It was only natural that a book written by Nitobe on morality would reflect his own religious beliefs. For example, on "politeness" (*rei*) Nitobe writes, "Politeness suffereth long, and is kind; envieth not, vaunteth not itself, is not puffed up; doth not behave itself unseemly, seeketh not her own, is not easily provoked, taketh not account of evil." This passage is almost identical to St. Paul's sermon about "love," in 1 Corinthians 13.

"Nitobe created a new religion," wrote the English Japanologist B.H. Chamberlain in his book *Things Japanese*. Without question, Nitobe's intention was to elucidate ethical teachings that were both new and eternal. He sought to emphasize that, although Christianity was by no means mainstream in Japan, a similar moral platform exists. He validated his point by drawing heavily on the philosophy and religion of the West, much more than the established treatises of Bushido written in the Edo period.

Chamberlain also took a personal potshot at Nitobe by calling him a "nationalist professor." In my view, he was very much an internationalist. Spending considerable time overseas, he was proud of his Japanese identity but not necessarily bound by traditional Japanese conventions. To call him a nationalist in the pejorative sense that Chamberlain intended was unfair. Even more unfair was that Nitobe's book would eventually become a propaganda tool in the militarist 1930s.

Bushido and Social Crisis

Japan developed an allergy to Bushido in the immediate postwar period. It was linked to the militarists and ultranationalists who sent Japan into a "death frenzy" of savagery, shame, and defeat. The renowned right-wing novelist Yukio Mishima (1915–70) thrust Bushido back into the limelight with his book *The Way of the Samurai*. In the text, he expounds on his own view of life and death as he explores the infamous Edo period book *Hagakure*. "*Hagakure* is the womb from which my writing is born . . . the eternal source of my vitality."

The Japanese sacrificed much during the war years, and, now truly repentant, they had somehow managed to divert that selfless loyalty to the point of death into selfless devotion to corporations (also sometimes to the death through overwork), which drove Japan's postwar economic recovery. A symbol of recovery was the 1964 Tokyo Olympic Games. Judo was made an Olympic sport for the first time in 1964.

This sparked renewed attention to Nitobe's book, particularly in light of Japan's return to favor in the international community. The world was amazed by Japan's speedy recovery from the rubble and ashes of its defeat less than two decades before.

Now over the postwar Bushido allergy, Japanese pundits were confident enough to address the elephant in the room. Could it be, they asked rhetorically, the spirit of Bushido still lurking in our Japanese DNA that enabled such rapid economic growth? An arbitrary summation maybe, but it was what citizens started to believe as Japan found its mojo again. Since the 1990s, however, following the catastrophic bursting of the economic bubble, people have continued to bemoan Japan's decline in national power. Once again, the cry goes out for Bushido as an answer to the country's social and economic ills. People are turning their attention to Bushido as a way of reinvigorating Japan. The current "Bushido boom" reflects a growing sense of domestic crisis in terms of the economy and the degradation of social values, and also its strained relations with neighboring powers. Bushido, it seems, never dies; it just finds new expressions to suit the times.

In this synopsis, I attempted to show how views of Bushido have changed over the centuries. As the understanding of Bushido evolves, so have the ways in which it has been utilized as a powerful emotive force—serving either as a humanistic guiding light for good or as a nationalistic cudgel for bad. Notwithstanding Bushido's exploitation for whatever agenda, it maintains a constant, enduring spirit with universal appeal. It is that very spirit, for example, that attracts so many around the world to study Japanese martial arts.

Still, most of the discourse on Bushido in Japan is based on Nitobe's rendition. His version of Bushido has become the basis of popular understanding; but we must not overlook the fact, although many do, that his dissertation was originally crafted to convince Westerners that predominantly non-Christian Japan was not a nation of morally depraved barbarians. He did not write it for a Japanese readership. It came back to Japan through a process of reverse engineering. This begs the question then: do Japanese people have any inkling of what Bushido really is? In fact, although I am a long-term martial arts practitioner and scholar of Japanese history and thought, it is a question that I have asked of myself for nearly three decades living in Japan. What the hell is Bushido, really? Does anybody know what Bushido is? Is it even possible that such a nebulous ideal, so fraught with castle-in-the-sky fantasies and contradictions, is really instilled in the psychological makeup of the Japanese people? My task in the next chapter is to tackle these questions.

CHAPTER 1

Zanshin: Lingering Mind and the Essence of Bushido

No Braggadocio in Budo

The 2012 Summer Olympics in London had plenty of drama, but one incident stands out in my memory: when Matsumoto Kaori won the gold medal in the women's judo lightweight (57 kg.) division. Her piercing gaze revealed her determination to win. The instant she was triumphant in the semifinal, ensuring her at least a bronze medal, she pumped her fist in a gesture the Japanese call a "guts pose." Apparently, this term was coined by the legendary Japanese boxer "Guts Ishimatsu," whose victory rituals endeared him to millions of fans. After Matsumoto's triumph in the final round, she shed tears of joy and flashed a V-for-victory sign to the cameras.

This was nothing out of the ordinary in international judo competition. Many, if not most, top athletes pump their fists in a defiant pose after clinching victory. Even Tani Ryoko, a two-time Olympic gold medalist and judo darling of Japan, customarily punched the air and jumped up and down as a way of expressing elation. Nobody can blame athletes for venting at the end of what was most likely a long, arduous journey to the top. They are simply letting go. Seeing displays of exultation also stirs something in spectators as they share the moment. After all, that is why people like to watch sports. It is all in the drama and the joy and despair at the end of the game. That said, such exhibitions are frowned upon in the world of budo.

If the vanquisher celebrated with a "guts pose" in a kendo match, for example, the point would be rescinded. In fact, depending on the level of immodesty demonstrated, the competitor may even be disqualified outright. Why? In kendo, openly revealing emotion in victory or defeat is considered rude. It shows a lack of *zanshin* and is at odds with the spirit of budo.

What, then, is *zanshin*? It is one of those Japanese budo terms best left as is, instead of trying to force an English equivalent. I usually translate it as "lingering mind." The first kanji (*zan*) means "remain," and the second (*shin*) is "heart." In other words, it describes a continued state of physical and psychological alertness after the engagement. It is not commonly heard in ordinary Japanese parlance. Few people other than martial arts (budo) aficionados ever encounter the word, but over my many years studying in Japan, I have come to understand that *zanshin* is a defining quality of Japanese budo. *Zanshin*, to my mind, therefore represents the "spirit of Bushido," the samurai warrior's code of ethics from which the spirit of the modern budo disciplines emanates.

True *zanshin* is not feigned. It is not just an act of keeping one's guard up. It is a physical and mental state of continuous vigilance that emerges after a decisive point has been scored. The budo mind is defined by the manifestation of *zanshin*. A martial artist who whoops with glee at the moment of victory may well be a superior athlete, but understands little about the ethos of Japanese budo and is no different from a soccer player celebrating a goal, or a sprinter cutting through the finish-line tape and blowing kisses to the crowd.

That is not to say that I am scornful of other sports and the antics of triumphant athletes. But an important part of budo is esteem of its traditions and respect for the people with whom you compete or train. Most athletes would say the same about their sport. However, budo has no room for egotistical displays of jubilance to rub salt into the wound of the opponent, or prancing about like a show pony in garish self-congratulatory rituals. Unfortunately, the kind of judo often seen at the Olympics, for example, falls outside the expected protocols of budo in this way. It is surely a fantastic competitive sport but has arguably forsaken the spirit of its roots and traditions as budo. More on this soon.

I was awoken to the implications of *zanshin* as the polestar of budo after decades of training in kendo (and other Japanese martial arts), and it has since become a fundamental consideration in how I live my life. More than anything else, *zanshin* has guided my personal quest to grow as a human being through the educational constructs of budo. In this chapter, I discuss what *zanshin* means from various angles and contemplate how budo provides a tangible path to the philosophical legacy of the samurai. How can this be tapped to enhance one's life experiences? I don't mean from the perspective of "I wanna be a samurai" but through utilizing pragmatic tenets of warrior wisdom that are carved into the masonry of the martial arts. That knowledge is there for the asking if you look in the right places.

Tighten Your Helmet Cords More in Victory

We are taught in kendo that, "When striking, always pay attention and never relax your guard." This is *zanshin* in its most basic form. Demonstrating *zanshin* means that the two competitors do not let up even after a match has been decided and the referees' flags are raised. To use a crude colloquialism, "It ain't over until the fat lady sings," and even if she does, it still ain't over. In other words, it is to remain eternally alert in both mind and in body to enable an instant response to any unexpected occurrence. *Zanshin* means never taking anything for granted. *Zanshin* is a concept with which martial artists develop a close affinity over time, as negligence will almost certainly result in injury or defeat. There is, however, so much more to it than this.

No one is quite sure just when and how the word came into being. It probably originated around the beginning of the Edo period (1603–1868) and pops up in several classical martial arts commentaries of the time. For example, in Yagyu Munenori's *Heiho-kadensho* (1632). "*Zanshin* / In attack and defense / To be orally transmitted." It is also in a selection of poems transmitting the secret teachings of Munenori's school of swordsmanship, Yagyu Shinkage-ryu: "Be mindful of *zanshin* in swordsmanship; do not be fooled by double-dealing counter techniques." And it is in another encoded poem from the Hozoin-ryu school of spearmanship, "First and foremost seek victory, but never forsake *zanshin*." From the same school: "*Zanshin* / Withdraw when enclosed at the front / Expect the unexpected." Teachings of the legendary sword master, Ito Ittosai (1560?–1653?), progenitor of the Itto-ryu school of swordsmanship, summarize the essence of *zanshin* as follows:

Zanshin is written with the characters for "remaining heart." Accordingly, under no circumstances should a warrior let down his guard believing that he has attained an emphatic victory. Even if there is outwardly no possibility that the enemy can recover after having the life stabbed or cut from him, one can never be too sure. It only takes a moment of negligence for a dramatic change of circumstance to cause one's own demise. This instruction remains as true now as it was in the old days. Never feel free from danger, even after you have taken your enemy's head. This continued state of alertness is the meaning of the teachings of *zanshin*.

Thus, the warrior's greatest enemy is his own loss of situational awareness. Victory is not the time to relax one's guard; it is a time to tighten the cords of your battle helmet. The same Itto-ryu scroll, however, also admonishes: "*Zanshin* [remaining heart] is not to leave any heart when the strike is made." This teaching seems to indicate the opposite of *zanshin* by attacking and leaving nothing behind. Leave the mind, or don't leave the mind? At a glance, it might seem to be a contradiction in terms, but this is testament to the multilayered complexion of *zanshin*. To make sense of it all, let us examine what happens in actual budo bouts today and how this spirit of *zanshin* lives on.

No *Zanshin*, No Point

Zanshin is a concept of mental and physical preparation common to all the martial arts. For example, in traditional Japanese archery (kyudo), *zanshin* is written two different ways: with the kanji for either "heart" or "body," both of which are pronounced *shin*. Archers are taught to maintain their concentration after the release, keep their bow in front, the rear arm exactly where it stops at the back after the release, and to follow the arrow with their eyes until it strikes its target. They maintain this pose for a few seconds before reticently preparing for the next shot. You cannot tell whether the arrow hit the target or not just by looking at the archer's expression and body language.

After a *kendoka* makes a strike, they remain vigilant and after opening up a safe amount of space between themselves and their opponent, turn to face them in preparation for another strike.

In karate and *iaido* (the art of sword drawing), *zanshin* is always seen at the end of kata. Kata are predetermined sequences of techniques in which an imagined aggressor or actual training partner is subdued and defeated. After each technique is executed, the one who theoretically wins the encounter will assume an en garde stance, measuring the distance between himself and the opponent, always ready to deliver a counterattack if needed. Never does one take one's eyes off the opponent, imaginary or real. In the case of *iaido*, it is only after this ritual that the blade can be sheathed to conclude the technique; but the right hand remains on the hilt ready to unleash fury again if the imaginary dead opponent should momentarily twitch back to life. Remember the *Terminator*?

In kendo, the feeling is the same, but the form is slightly different. *Kendoka* (kendo practitioners) are trained such that, after a target has been struck, they follow through still primed and ready to go. What you think was a valid point might be only a glancing flesh wound in the eyes of the referees. Their flags will stay down, and the chances are high that the opponent is already launching a counterattack just as you realize you will not be awarded any points. Nothing is more embarrassing than walking back to the start line thinking that you scored, only to be "unexpectedly" struck in kind with a blow that the judges deem valid. After striking the opponent, the *kendoka* immediately prepares to strike again, irrespective of whether the initial point was ruled valid. The "fat lady sings" only after the head referee officially proclaims the justness of the point in gesture and word. Even then, *zanshin* is paramount for reasons that I will explain shortly.

Kendo matches are decided on the best of three points scored on four possible target areas: the head (*men*), torso (*do*), wrists (*kote*), and the throat (*tsuki*). Matches have three referees, and a technique is validated if two of them raise their flags for the red or white player. The first *kendoka* to score two valid points wins the match. It is not enough for the sword merely to touch the target area. The rules that must be satisfied have stringent criteria. A valid point is awarded only after an accurate strike or thrust is made on designated targets using the "striking section" (sweet spot) of the bamboo sword with the blade in the correct cutting angle. The strike or thrust must be executed in "high spirits" with "correct posture," unity of body, mind and sword, and then followed by *zanshin*.

Even the most beautifully executed, palpable technique will not be counted if, in the opinion of the referees, the *kendoka* does not demonstrate *zanshin*. The referees wait a second or two before they indicate their decision to confirm the contender's behavior after the attack. Thus, the "point" is not decided at the "point" of impact; the referees are looking at intent, contact, form, and then physical and psychological composure, leading back to the intent stage again. In other words, rather than a point, it is a process that is being judged.

Poker Face

How do the judges know whether competitors have shown the proper *zanshin*? I find this is easier to teach to students not familiar with kendo through videos. For this purpose, I often use the final of the fifty-third All-Japan Kendo Championship in 2005. There is no reason I use this example over anything else, other than that I was courtside at the time and caught the final moment with my handy-cam.

The winner of this final bout was destined to be crowned the champion of Japan. The two opponents bowed to each other and then faced off in the en garde stance waiting for the head referee to proclaim the start of the match. The match progressed with plenty of exciting tit-for-tat attacks, but neither could gain any advantage and satisfy the requirements to raise the referees' flags in their favor.

Because no points were scored by the end of the designated match time, it went to a sudden death round. The first to score one point would be the new champion of Japan. Then, white coaxed red into making a strike to his head (*men*). Having initiated the attack by making red think there was an opening to be had, white deftly nipped the start of the men-strike in the bud and took out red's wrist (*kote*) just as he lifted his hands to reach out. White kept his sword pointed at red as he moved out of the way, ensuring that red could not follow up. He was not looking at the three white flags that the referees had raised. Instead, he was intently staring at his opponent, making sure that all danger was past.

Meanwhile, red, acknowledging that his *kote* had been struck and that he could not now make a counterattack, bowed his head to white as a sign of submission and respect. The head referee announced the successful *kote* point. The match was over. Each competitor carefully returned to the face-off lines. Not for a second did either of them lower his gaze or lose eye contact as they crouched down in sync, sheathed their bamboo swords, retreated to either side of the match area, bowed, and then vacated the match court.

Although white had struck red's wrist, it is hard for the uninitiated to discern who won because the attempted *men* strike and the successful *kote* strike were executed simultaneously. If you blink, you miss it. Furthermore, in ideal kendo form, it was impossible to tell which side had won after the fact because both had their emotions completely in check, with no display of elation or disappointment, no smiles nor tears—just the same deadpan expression on both their faces.

In kendo circles, becoming the champion of Japan is an honor on a par with winning an Olympic gold medal. For the winner, this is undoubtedly the culmination of a childhood dream and long years of grueling practice. In any other sport, it would be completely ordinary, even expected for the winner to dance a little jig of joy. It would be just as pedestrian for the loser to curse the heavens for his rotten luck or spout poisonous barbs at the referees for their "bad call."

This is not the case with kendo though. The loser shows no annoyance whatsoever. Doing so would be indefensibly disrespectful to the opponent and the spirit of kendo—sacrilege. He simply acknowledges his defeat and bows. He had a chink in his armor on which his opponent capitalized. Even if the judgment was dubious, there is a reason the call went against him that is most likely rooted in own actions and mind-set. Now he has something to work on in his training. Defeat has a silver lining.

The winner, likewise, will never boast. He may have won but humbly acknowledges that it was by no means a perfect victory. Sure, as in all sports a win is a win, and we certainly do not compete in kendo to lose! The *kendoka*, however, is expected always to seek improvement, and competitions are a vehicle for this. Winning is not the ultimate objective per se. Learning about your strengths and weaknesses is. Match results provide tangible checkpoints along the path of personal development. Both winners and losers show no emotion as they exit the arena. This makes it a boring affair for professional photographers trying to capture telltale expressions of jubilation and despair. Both just thank each other again and head back to the dojo to resume training (maybe stopping off for a quick beer on the way).

This attitude is prescribed in the "Budo Charter" of the Japanese Budo Association. The association is the collective of nine modern budo disciplines recognized by the Japanese government: kendo, judo, *kyudo* (archery), aikido, karate, sumo, *shorinji kempo*, *naginata* (glaive), and *jukendo* (bayonet). When training in budo, practitioners must "resist the temptation to pursue mere technical skill rather than strive towards the perfect unity of mind, body and technique" (Article 2, Training). Article 3, which outlines the correct attitude for competition, states that competitors "must do their best at all times, winning with modesty, accepting defeat gracefully, and constantly exhibiting self-control." This is *zanshin*.

The Consequences of Crowing

If the referees have misgivings about how a bout is proceeding, the match is suspended, and the three of them confer at center court while the two fighters crouch down and wait for the result of the deliberation. Referees have the option of rescinding a proclaimed point if a mistake has clearly been made. As I mentioned above, *zanshin* is an essential requirement of a valid point. Without it, a point should not be awarded even if the strike itself was perfect. Even a tiny fist pump is enough for a point to be cancelled. It is looked upon as a sign of disrespect and arrogance and shows a lack of *zanshin*.

Another video I use frequently in my classes shows a high school team match in the final round of a prefectural championship. The red and white teams, each made up of five fighters, had won two matches apiece. It was down to the final bout between the captains to decide their team's fate. Red drew first blood with a successful strike to white's wrist. White needed to score next or lose. The pressure was on, but white managed to make an incredibly dexterous attack on red's wrist to bring the match back to even at one point each. As both captains were returning to the face-off lines to duel it out for the decider, white turned to his teammates and made a very discreet celebratory gesture out of relief that he was still in the match. The referees, seeing this, gathered at center court and determined that white had indeed pumped his fist toward his teammates. As concealed and low key as it was, white's action was still judged "disrespectful," and his hard-earned point was nullified on account of his unemphatic indiscretion. This harsh verdict is typical of kendo.

My own teammate once launched a spectacular strike on the torso of his opponent. It was so powerful that he could not stop the momentum and pirouetted on the spot—a devastating hit and then some. The technique was beautiful, but the result was … zilch! Spinning around in the follow through, he inadvertently turned his back on his adversary. The referees initially raised their flags but then came the dreaded huddle. Although he had not done it on purpose, the point was rescinded. We were told later that, intentionally or not, it is rude to turn one's back on one's opponent, and it "showed a lack of *zanshin*." Point taken.

No "No Mind"

A story of one of my failures is instructive as to whether *zanshin* is present. In the fall of 2004, a competition was held in Kyoto for company teams. Although not a company employee, I was appointed as the captain of a printing company team with whom I often trained. Our five-member team was in top form, and we were doing well in the matches. In the quarter-final, we had one win, two losses, and one draw. I was the last to fight, and I needed to defeat my opponent by two points to force a playoff. Everything was riding on my bout.

My opponent was a formidable fencer, but I was resolved to give it my all and let the result take care of itself. Not far into the bout, I managed to score a strike to his head—a decisive hit. I felt no particular emotion, no desire or excitement after taking the lead. I was in the zone. Then, before I knew it, I had scored a second point to his head. I had won against a veritable local hero, and the crowd went wild. My victory meant a playoff between a representative from each team. That match would be sudden death: the first to score one point would win.

There is no rule saying the captain must be the one to fight, but my team members decided for me. This was a hefty responsibility. When I learned that I had the same opponent, clearly intent on revenge and restoring his honor, I let it get to me. Where was that state of "no mind" (*mushin*) that I managed to drift into just a few moments before? With this sudden flood of worries, attachments, fears, and mundane thoughts polluting my mind, the result of my final bout was predictably disastrous. My opponent made short work of me with a whack to the wrist. Having won my initial bout, I fatally thought that my work was done. I lacked *zanshin*. The principles of *zanshin* are simple. Never relax your guard, no matter what, and don't let things mess with your head. If I had only been able to remember that … It was a painful experience because I crumbled under pressure. I was my own worst enemy.

Hung Up on Winning

The presence or absence of *zanshin* is sometimes revealed when referees make a bad call. I am reminded of the judo competition at the 2000 Sydney Olympics. In the 100-kg. and over class, Shinohara Shin'ichi was paired against David Douillet of France in the final round. In what is widely regarded in Japan as the "worst misjudgment in judo history," the two of them fell to the ground, and Shinohara pumped his fists in the air, claiming an *ippon*—a full point that would have ended the match. Instead, Shinohara was awarded only a lesser score (*yuko*). In the end, it was Douillet who came away triumphant.

I have it on good authority from a very experienced Japanese judoka, Nakajima Takeshi, that the call differs depending on the angle from which it is viewed. This observation puts him in a minority in Japan. Moreover, the fact that the head referee was my compatriot leaves me open to accusations of bias. *Ippon* or *yuko* aside, what bothered me about the match was what happened afterward. Taking his camcorder to the officials, Japan's head coach, Yamashita Yasuhro, complained long and loud that the referees had made a terrible mistake.

Yamashita is a genuine folk hero in Japan, and the gold medal he won at the 1984 Los Angeles Olympics in the prestigious open weight category is still talked about today. To the bitter end, this great judoka was making a mockery of judo and its traditions with his behavior. Ironically, the Japanese commentator on television backed Yamashita's crusade to the hilt, calling the referees a disgrace and saying that *their* behavior was an affront to judo traditions.

Sometime later, Douillet wrote a letter to Yamashita along the following lines. "I love the spirit of judo, and for a long time now I have held you in the greatest esteem, Mr. Yamashita. It is thus that I have a sense of regret that your passionate appeal of the Olympic referees' decision was in violation of the budo spirit." I had an opportunity to talk with Yamashita about this. "Behaving as I did is one of my greatest regrets," he said. "I really learned my lesson."

I was impressed with the sincerity of Yamashita's response. Screwing up is a part of the developmental process. We all do it. I believe it was his humility that made him the world's premier judoka in his day. Starting in 2001, Yamashita became the central figure in the "Judo Renaissance" movement, which aimed to revive interest in the educational thinking of its founder, Kano Jigoro. Credit is due to Shinohara as well. In his post-match comment, he said, "I lost because I was weak." Most pundits in Japan, however, did not see it this way.

Since judo became an event contested at the Olympics in 1964, many traditionalists lament how it has forsaken its educational ideals of personal development in the quest for Olympic glory, competition, and commercialism. Standing on the podium to receive a medal has, many bemoan, become the main objective. It is the result that counts, rather than the process. This is the juncture at which sports and budo supposedly head in different directions. Once the prototypical modern budo, is judo now a sport?

How do *kendoka* react when faced with a questionable decision by referees? *Kendoka* can usually tell when a judgment is wrong, especially when they are on the receiving end. No matter what their own opinion might be, they abide dutifully by the decision of the judges. The loser bows and says, "I concede." They never express any doubt about referee calls. Why? A point is declared when two or more of the three referees independently raise their flags in favor. If a close decision goes against you, it is because there was something off in your kendo in the eyes of the referees.

In the arena of competition, you must be able to persuade the referees that your technique is valid or, conversely, that the opponent's technique is not, regardless of angle from which it is viewed. This is demonstrated not through words or gestures, but through your movement, posture, composure, stance, striking opportunities, and *zanshin*. In other words, the onus is on you as the competitor to "strike the referees' hearts" as well as the opponent, not on the referee to give you the benefit of the doubt.

It is all about attitude. In kendo, it is said: "You may win some by good fortune, but you don't lose through bad fortune." There is always a reason, and it lies within you, which is why there is no room for complaint. Of course, no one wants to lose, and to be beaten because of an error in judgment is certainly hard to take. The question, however, is if you lose because of a referee's error, what do you take away from that? Is there a lesson in there somewhere? If there isn't, then you are not looking hard enough. Of course, winning and losing are important, but so is comporting oneself in a dignified manner and not doing anything shameful. This is also a kind of *zanshin*. Being a practicing *kendoka* is de rigueur for refs, so they, too, are learning hard lessons in that their judgments reflect their own level of kendo.

The Concealed "Guts Pose"

What happened to *zanshin* in judo? Bitter-enders in Japan often blame the perceived "devolution" of judo from budo to nothing more than a "wrestling competition in pajamas" because it was "internationalized." Judo is criticized as having sold its soul to commercialization and adherence to the doctrine that victory is everything. Kano Jigoro, the founder of judo, "would surely be turning over in his grave," they cry. Budo disciplines such as *kyudo* and aikido, by contrast, continue to place greater emphasis on tradition than on competition. Kendo falls somewhere in between, but does that mean that kendo is a "purer" form of budo than judo? Many *kendoka* would say yes. "Judo is not budo because it has lost its *zanshin*..."

The truth, however, is that even kendo has been losing its *zanshin*. More than a few *kendoka* think of *zanshin* simply as a matter of form, just taking a stance that makes you look ready, but with nothing behind it. Worse, some can be seen pumping the bamboo sword in the air, rather than their fist. It would be their fist if they did not have a sword in both hands! I have observed even top-ranked, eighth-*dan kendoka* do things that make me wonder whether they understand what *zanshin* truly is. Watching some college students practice kendo, I frequently want to cover my eyes. Just their body language shows they are doing everything but the pumping. The culpability lies with their instructors for failing to teach their students what *zanshin* really is.

What is so wrong about expressing honest emotions? Some say that fist pumping is a hardwired, instinctive human gesture, and not something to criticize. My friend David Matsumoto, a former US judo coach and a professor of psychology at San Francisco State University, reported in his research that great joy is often accompanied by a surge of adrenalin that causes the body to rigidify. "Triumph has its own signature expression that is immediate, automatic and universal across cultures." Pumping one's fists in the air is a reflex that anybody could experience in the throes of intense excitement.

This may be so, but, as with many instinctive actions, the challenge for humans is to learn how to channel and control their behavior, physically, mentally, and spiritually. To be human is to learn how to keep our instincts and emotions in check. *Zanshin* is a teaching by which we foster such control. *Zanshin* is such control. *Zanshin* was the basis of vitality in Bushido (Way of the samurai). By virtue of this, *zanshin* is the lifeblood of budo (martial arts).

Learning through Losing

At the London Olympics, Japan won thirty-eight medals—more than ever before. But, for the first time, Japan failed to win a gold medal in men's judo. Japan's medal count of seven was tied with France's in the judo events—a result regarded by Japanese media and viewers as "humiliating." The Japanese judoka returned home disheartened and to little fanfare. This reaction meant that, in spite of judo's often touted values of goodwill, humility, and respect, the number of medals attained, and associated national prestige, trumps all. This reaction was another indication that Olympic judo is now more a competitive sport than a bastion of budo spirit.

The expectation of the media and the average Japanese person in the street for international dominance and a mini-gold rush filled my head with irreconcilable thoughts, not least the brazen contradiction of it all. The decline of budo values in judo is too often blamed on its international dissemination and the negative forces of globalization. But the most stalwart preachers of budo ideals in Japan unashamedly succumb to the media hype and superficial attitude that anything other than "Kimigayo" (Japanese national anthem) blaring from the speakers at the awards ceremony is a disgrace when national honor is on the line.

An emblematic variation between the attitude in budo and competitive sports is that, while both are concerned with winning and losing, budo puts a higher priority on self-control before, during, and after the bout. It is not only about whether you win or lose, but "how" you win or lose. What does this mean exactly?

For winners, *zanshin* is keeping your guard up, keeping cool, calm and collected, and maintaining a sense of humility. Post-match merriment expressed by high-fiving, posing, twerking, kissing, and hugging your teammates is sufficient evidence of a *zanshin* void. At the same time—and this is important—there is also *zanshin* for losers. Actually, there is no distinction. We are usually focused on the deportment of winners, but should also pay attention to whether those who lose are exhibiting the right attitude.

For a loser to lose his cool and slam his sword on the floorboards or to sob and crumble in an inconsolable temper tantrum is unthinkable in budo. Throwing one's toys out of the crib like a spoiled child, or even letting that telltale tear of internal devastation roll down your cheek is as every bit as inappropriate in the budo setting as jumping for joy. A good loser holds his sorrow, anger, frustration, and resentment in a headlock and learns to choke it. At the end of the bout, he simply concedes with gratitude, "I lost," and steps back with poise and self-esteem intact.

In budo, as with anything in life, many things can be learned from being on the losing end. "I was struck on the head. He taught me that I was open somewhere, and I have to figure out the root of the weakness. Is it technical, or is it mental?" Usually, the two are inextricably linked. These lessons help me to focus in my ensuing practice sessions. My opponent has given me homework that, ultimately, if I have the right attitude, will contribute greatly to my development as a *kendoka* and, by extension, as a human being.

Failure is the grist for growing stronger. It is a process of purging one's mind of weaknesses, identifying chinks in one's spiritual armor, and filling the gaps with cold hard lessons from defeat. These lessons are what we thank our opponents for after the match is over. The pre- and post-match ritual of bowing in deference to one's opponent, notwithstanding the result, is probably the most fundamental imperative in all budo disciplines for this very reason. We humans, being emotional animals, may find it difficult to thank our vanquisher (and vice versa) with a genuine feeling of gratitude. If done habitually at the beginning and end of every encounter, it becomes an embodied value over time in which one truly believes.

This is what is meant by *shugyo* (austere training)—the designation for the "study" of budo. It is a lifelong journey of bloody hard work, sucking it up, and self-reflection. For *shugyo* to be possible in budo, you need an opponent who is going to push you in competition and regular training. Your opponent is not your enemy; he or she is a collaborator on a mutual path of self-improvement. Opponents teach you that the biggest obstacle is not them, but yourself. Thank goodness for opponents.

A Dictum for Survival

Think of *zanshin* as the competition that takes place after the match is over. The moment of impact in a budo match is only half the battle. The other half comes after the blow. Win or lose, a *kendoka* is taught never to take anything for granted. No exuberance. No downheartedness. Always calm, perceptive, and mindful after the fact. Showing an awareness of one's surroundings, humility, consideration, and empathy to one's adversary in victory and gratitude in defeat are elements of *zanshin*. It is not just about getting ready for counterattacks.

I believe that *zanshin* is the essence of budo. Such a polished state of mental and physical preparedness stems from samurai experiences in mortal combat. Of course, modern kendo is different in many ways from the sword-fighting in which samurai combatants of old engaged, but its technical and philosophical origins emanate from there. *Zanshin* is a central principle conveyed over generations of swordsmen that equates to the difference between living or dying.

After the *kendoka* makes a thrust or strike, the momentum generated in the forward lunging motion allows him to follow through and create space in order to ready himself for the next exchange of blows. In the days of dueling with live blades—giant 30-inch razors—even a glancing blow from a felled enemy convulsing in a pool of blood could be your undoing. Human beings somehow have an incredible propensity to summon their last bit of strength to accomplish one final superhuman feat. In a modern kendo match, a strike to the wrist is good enough for victory, but samurai lore passed down through the ages teaches us that having a severed hand does not mean defeat. After all, there is still one good hand left. And a jagged stump is sufficient for a good punch in the face.

If the enemy appears to have given up the ghost, it may well be a trick to entice you to drop your guard. A Japanese poem says: "Relax not the mind at any time / The wind that brings the mountain cherry blossoms also takes them away." Idiomatic of Japan's natural beauty, cherry trees are gorgeous when in full bloom. When picking up a handful of fallen petals from the lush pink carpet underfoot, one admires their delicate beauty and fragrance. Then a sudden gust of spring wind blows them from your hand. Victory is the same. It may seem as if you have it firmly in your grasp, but the unexpected can happen when you feel secure, and then all will be lost.

Warrior dissertations admonish fighting men never to let up. Even if the enemy's head is severed from his neck, it would be ludicrous to let rip with a fist pump or little victory dance. As the warrior reveled in his exploit, he would be oblivious to another opponent sneaking up from behind to take his own head. When life is at stake, samurai were warned, continued attentiveness is the key to survival. Even now, *zanshin* fits the bill as the ultimate lesson for prevailing in any environment.

Zanshin and the Duel at Ganryujima

Still on the topic of *zanshin*, I would like to examine the famous duel at Ganryujima in 1612 between two renowned swordsmen: Miyamoto Musashi (1584–1685) and Sasaki Kojiro (1585?–1612). Day and time

A man holds up a magnifying glass to look at the famous samurai swordsman Miyamoto Musashi. (*Miyamoto Musashi* by Utagawa Kuniyoshi [Between 1847 and 1850] Retrieved from the Library of Congress, www.loc.gov/item/2002700026/)

decided, Kojiro awaited Musashi's arrival at the appointed island, Ganryujima. Showdown time came, but Musashi did not. Kojiro grew irate. This is when Musashi made his grand entry.

Yoshikawa Eiji dramatized this episode in his popular prewar novel about Musashi, which is well known to all Japanese. It is impossible to know how much historical truth stands behind the actual circumstances. The duel was a private affair between the two warriors and was not sanctioned by the rulers of the Hosokawa domain, where the place of battle took place. Leaving questions of historical authenticity aside, as the story has usually been told for the past couple of hundred years, Musashi was the superior swordsman both tactically and psychologically, but not necessarily technically. The dueling process was not just about skill in swordwork but was very much a game of wits. Kojiro lost his, and was defeated before the duel even kicked off.

Musashi had just one thought in mind: winning. Although revered as swordsman supreme in Japan, Musashi was not without his critics. He has always had detractors who chastise him as a sly dog who would stop at nothing to win, even resorting to less-than-gentlemanly conduct akin to cowardice. It is said that he engaged in over sixty life-and-death duels and never lost. He was clearly not a coward in his willingness to test himself in the couldron of combat. The criticism comes from the way in which he went about winning.

Arriving late to upset his adversary's state of mind was a brilliant stratagem, if the goal is to win at any price. If he had squared off against Kojiro in a fair fight as agreed upon, he might well have lost. From the perspective of the spirit of martial arts, even then, it was incumbent on Musashi to fight, dare I say, with a spirit of sportsmanship. This was no time for vague or sneaky stratagems—they just would not do.

If it is true that Musashi's tardiness threw Kojiro off his game, one must conclude that Kojiro was spiritually no match for Musashi. Another possibility is that he thought to himself, "Musashi is a sloppy pratt. I will win because I am an upstanding dude who plays by the rules." In that case, Kojiro's arrogance led to his undoing. The outcome might have been very different had he kept his emotions in check before reacting. Kojiro, too, was wanting in *zanshin*.

At the end of his life, Musashi retreated to a cave and recorded his martial wisdom for posterity in five scrolls (*Gorin-no-sho*). In it, Musashi confesses that, after turning thirty, he came to the Zen-like realization that strategy was more than just a matter of winning and losing, and thus considered his life to that point as having been on the wrong path. He survived, he admitted, simply through good luck, rather than any prodigious understanding of universal wisdom.

Contrition and Compassion

Bushido and the martial arts in general have an exceedingly macho image. In fact, one of the early appellations for the warrior's path in Japan was *dando*, or the "manly way." Sometimes, Bushido is associated with reckless brutality and atrocities fueled by unbridled testosterone and an utter disrespect for life. Inspection of countless historical sources, however, reveals in a most unambiguous way that the ideal warrior was one who forged strength tempered with compassion and empathy. I look at this dichotomy in more detail in Chapter 2.

To reiterate, *zanshin* is not just controlling emotion or surviving by keeping your wits about you. A kendo teacher taught me once:

"*Zanshin* is to have a heart of contriteness." He meant that *zanshin*, in addition to being a survival mechanism, is also a lesson in humanity. To defeat an adversary in battle is to take his life. War or not, the taking of life is homicide—a morally reprehensible act in all cultures if it can be avoided. One who kills simply for pleasure represents the purest manifestation of the dormant evil that resides in every single one of us. *Zanshin*—lingering heart—in this sense, has yet another deeper spiritual connotation. It is the "contrite heart," which might also be described as the "compassionate heart." Compassion (*jihi*) is a word often used in Buddhist discourse but is an absolute virtue throughout all of humankind. If empathy is putting yourself in other's shoes, compassion represents the instinctive get-up-and-go to help. Rejoicing over a defeated opponent points to a compassionless heart—a total degeneration of humanity.

Fallen foes deserve the utmost respect and compassion. When you fight for your life, you are true to your convictions, whatever they may be. The basis for all human action, for all convictions, is survival. If not your own, then those who share the same convictions. A mortal enemy in the throes of combat is no different in this sense. Your ideologies may be polar opposites, but your conviction is the same; and it is the enemy's conviction, not his cause, with which the warrior empathizes. Victory may mean the continuation of your cause for a little longer, but it could very easily be you slumped in the blood-soaked dirt. To the samurai, death was the time to reflect on the value of life—a time that, in addition to being thankful to be alive, the warrior was grateful to his enemy for showing him this.

Even if a cause can be justified—something that is always subjective—killing is still nothing to be proud of. The combatant goes into a frenzy amid the slaughter. In the melee, the samurai learned that he must somehow keep intact the thin thread of humanity that, once broken, would end in a rapid descent to hell. In this sense, *zanshin* is a reminder not to forget humanity. Although light years away from the realities of war, the bow performed at the beginning and the end of each bout in kendo symbolizes this realization. Are we, budo forces us to ask, animals or human beings? Strict protocols of etiquette have always been a feature of Japanese budo precisely because of the horrors experienced in war.

The Depth of Bowing

Let us return to the London Olympics in 2012. The semifinal match in women's soccer was between Japan and France. After Japan won that match, the Japanese captain, Miyama Aya, went over to console a French player who sat crying on the pitch. She softly put her hand on her shoulder in a gesture that was widely eulogized in Japan as a beautiful show of sports[wo]manship. The Japanese media jumped on the scene as one of the high points of the Olympics. Watching it at a local sports bar, I felt as if, more than respect or sympathy, what Miyama was showing was genuine empathy for her opponent.

Empathy, the ability to understand another person's thinking without judgment, stands at the core of rituals of gratitude in budo. An awful lot of bowing occurs in a dojo, perhaps more than at any other venue in Japan. We express gratitude and respect to our teachers with a bow at the beginning and end of training. This is an extension of the deference to those who pioneered our path—previous generations of martial artists who go back centuries and who have bequeathed to us their bloodstained wisdom in an unbroken chain. In practice bouts or competitions, however, although it is the standard interpretation the bow is not one of respect. To be more precise, the ultimate declaration is of respect, but the heart of the bow is premised on empathy, symbolizing equality and the promise that we hold no animosity, come what may.

The bow is the alpha and omega of budo. The "please" we say as we bow before a fight, and the "thank you" we say while bowing after, are both grounded in empathy. The bow is an expression of the realization that one of us will figuratively, possibly even literally, die here. Each one is hoping to come out on top, but nobody knows who it will be, until that person retreats courteously from the court. After ten years of hard training, the decisive blow is over in 0.3 seconds. Anything can happen.

Our positions are equal as we face off. Because we are equal, we hold no enmity for each other, only an unspoken understanding. Our minds and skills might be on different planes, but our hearts are on the same page. With empathy at its nucleus, bowing and the various protocols of etiquette characteristic of budo are an affirmation of respect and constitute a profoundly deep form of communication that transcends gender, age, color, creed, and religion.

Eye Contact

When bowing, it is important to maintain eye contact. Peering into each other's eyes, we observe the entirety of the opponent, like "looking at a distant mountain." The metal grill on a kendo mask has a slightly

Maintaining eye contact with my opponent during a match (2014).

wider gap where the eyes are positioned. The eyes are the only unimpeded feature on the opponent's face. They are windows into the soul.

The use of eyes when communicating in Japan is sometimes confusing. The term *me-ue*, which means "eyes above," is used in reference to one's superiors. In the rigid hierarchy of Japanese society, most people feel uncomfortable looking someone in the eye when they converse, especially if the other person is higher up in the pecking order. In budo, however, looking one's adversary in the eye is required as a matter of courtesy. When bowing to the shrine in a dojo, it is considered proper etiquette to bend 30° from the waist with eyes cast downward. Before a bout, however, the norm is to bow 15° while looking each other in the eye. The second you take your eyes off your opponent in the clamor, you leave yourself open. You cannot afford to give your opponent an inch. Again, this is an intrinsic idea behind *zanshin*.

When bowing from the kneeling position, you slide both hands simultaneously down the thighs onto the floor to form a triangle with the thumbs and forefingers touching in front of your knees. A bow of 90° is conducted with the nose positioned above the triangle, keeping the back and neck straight. (This prevents a broken nose and enables you to breath if somebody slams your head to the floor from behind.) The eyes are lowered to the floor at the last possible moment and then raised to look straight at the opponent as soon as the upper body is raised.

Another way to bow is to place the left hand on the floor slightly before the right and then, when concluding the bow, draw the right hand back up the thigh first. The reason is that the Japanese sword is unsheathed with the right hand, so you must be prepared to draw it at any moment by leaving the right hand in place for as long as possible. Training the mind and body to be ready for an attack at any time even during the ceremonial bow of respect—in other words, regarding the encounter as deadly serious—is an expression of sincerity and discipline. Eye contact is also an expression of compassion. This becomes even more poignant after the opponent's defeat. Thus, looking the opponent in the eye communicates caution, whereas averting one's gaze is not only careless but a denial of the empathetic bond. Breaking eye contact in budo is viewed as underhanded and cowardly.

Zanshin outside the Dojo

How can *zanshin* be applied outside the context of budo? The possibilities are endless. In mountaineering, for example, danger is ever present. A friend who enjoys climbing once told me that eighty percent of accidents occur not on the ascent but the descent. Climbers have a keen sense of vulnerability as they inch their way to the summit. They understandably feel elated upon reaching the top, but the real danger comes when they relax on the way back down. They are in extreme danger of feeling that they have won the battle, and this is when they slip and fall to their death: catastrophic *zanshin* breakdown.

For mountaineers, reaching the peak is not the goal. The goal is making it back to basecamp after an arduous journey up and then back down again. In this sense, climbing a mountain has many similarities to kendo. The point is how one acts after reaching the summit—or scoring a point in kendo—and then following through with even more vigilance and tightening those helmet cords. Not doing so is inviting tragedy.

Knowing *zanshin* allows us to live well in a variety of ways. For example, taking care of one's health is a form of *zanshin*. Showing consideration to friends and strangers is another. If we had *zanshin* at work, we might not have to do so much overtime, and careless mistakes would be greatly reduced. For the budo practitioner, it is through putting *zanshin* to use in everyday life that we begin to see its true significance.

People lose their keys, leave their wallet or phone at the bar, forget to flush the toilet. Minor mishaps like this are all *zanshin*-less slipups. Usually it is no big deal, and things may turn out okay, but a splash of *zanshin* makes life so much easier. We all forget trivialities on occasion, but this can lead to disproportionate catastrophes. No *zanshin* in the context of daily life is born of a failure to create a little buffer of space, stepping back and taking a minute to refocus, pay attention, and get back in the moment.

Although the word itself is not mentioned, Bushido classics such as *Hagakure*, *Koyo-gunkan*, and *Chikubasho* all relay how crucial it is to be constantly aware of one's circumstances and surroundings, even more so in peace. *Hagakure*, for example, contains instructions for acting appropriately at drinking parties. Samurais liked to party but careless imbibing could have "grave" consequences.

> One should always be careful to behave properly at social gatherings. Careful observation of revelries show that the majority are resigned to getting totally drunk. Partaking in alcohol is pleasurable so long as one ceases consumption at an appropriate time. It looks vulgar if one behaves recklessly, and it is an indication of one's character and [low] level of refinement. When drinking, the warrior should be aware that eyes are always upon him. Act appropriately in public.

The *Hagakure* admonition is still perfectly relevant three centuries later and is certainly not a startling piece of advice. In the time of the samurai, however, drunken shenanigans could easily end up in bloodshed. The victims friends or family members may seek to "even the score," and a little fun could literally end up with the town being painted red.

Zanshin means never losing control, no matter what, and knowing when to stop and go home (by taxi, of course). Also, getting a receipt from the driver as you disembark is prudent insurance *zanshin*, just in case you forget your satchel in the cab. That way, you will know which company to contact and will be able to cancel out your careless lack of *zanshin* with a "get out of jail" *zanshin* card!

All or Nothing

At the beginning of this chapter, I cited a scroll from the Itto-ryu school of swordsmanship. *Zanshin* means continued mindfulness after an attack, but it is also true that the swordsman must forget the mind when striking. Does this mean we should leave the mind behind? The message itself is a kind of parable—"mindlessness" (*mushin*) versus "mindfulness" (*zanshin*).

Sometimes, in kendo, teachers cite the following analogy to explain *zanshin*:

> Upon filling a cup with water and then quickly tipping it out in a swift motion, the cup will not be dry inside as drops of liquid will cling to the sides and bottom. Throwing it out with all of your might is what enables some water to remain.

In terms of swordplay, when we strike an opponent with all our heart, residue remains naturally for the same reason. This will not happen if the strike is hesitant or halfhearted. In that case, no momentum will be generated, and as the technique fizzles to its inevitable floppy end, mind and body will be unable to follow through to the second or even third move as required. Only striking with one's whole heart, forgetting the self, sacrificing the body, will result in a successful strike or the ability to keep the initiative going.

Shingitai = Coalescence of mind, technique, and body

The circular nature of *zanshin* as mind, body, and technique coalesce.

That is why *kendoka* are often told that to "leave the heart," you must first "strike without leaving the heart." We are taught to strike with our whole heart in a state of no-mindedness (*mushin*), that is, devoid of discursive thought, judgment, and desire. Only then, requirements for a decisive blow in kendo, with residual water still in the cup, can we continue to the next stage. *Zanshin* is like a semicolon; it finishes one stanza but links it to the next. A strike in kendo, then, is not a point in time but a continuous circle; and *zanshin* is the beginning, middle, and end.

An important consideration here is that striking with one's whole heart does not mean that the bamboo sword is swung around like a mass murderer's axe. The mind, body, and sword are all deployed in unison, as one consolidated entity. Power for the strike is generated with a degree of physical strength, but not too much. The bamboo sword is wielded lightly, with subtle movements of the shoulders, arms, wrists, and palms, and the body is driven forward by the legs and hips all perfectly coordinated.

As a comparison, people who play Japanese drums (*taiko*) do not strike the drum with every ounce of their physical strength, lest they put the stick through the drumhead. They beat the drum with just the right physical intensity and flexibility, with a snap of the wrists. The drumstick rebounds naturally back to the ready position to strike again. You can see that they are totally at one with the drum. They do not think about the sequence of movements and coordinating the connection of sinews and muscles. If they did, the drumming would stop.

In his 1641 treatise "Heiho-sanjugokajo" (35 Articles on the Art of Swordsmanship), Miyamoto Musashi took up the subject of *zanshin* and *hoshin* (liberation from tenacious thoughts):

> Whether to allow the heart to linger [*zanshin*] or let it go [*hoshin*] is dependent on the objective and circumstances. With sword in hand, it is advisable to release the conscious heart and hold back the subconscious heart. The instant you

strike the enemy with intent, release the conscious heart and hold back the subconscious heart. The method for holding back [*zanshin*] or letting go [*hoshin*] is contingent on various factors. This should be studied well.

When we speak of *zanshin*, it is not born of a conscious intention to "leave heart." This just causes hesitation and confusion and will stymie decisive action. Consciously leaving heart amounts to half-heartedness. Wholehearted resolve to sacrifice everything into the strike results in the heart remaining as a natural byproduct of total conviction to the task. It cannot be forced. The concept was expressed rather arcanely by Ito Ittosai using the Buddhist term *fusho-fumetsu*: "The secret way of the sword 'neither arising nor ceasing' lies in the teaching of *zanshin*." This alludes to the idea of enlightenment through the way of the sword.

We are prone to dwell on our limitations. "If I use eighty percent of my strength, twenty percent will remain. If I use 100 percent, there will be nothing left at all." Is that really the case? If twenty percent is consciously left over, new strength will not spring forth. It is only when the swordsman has pushed himself beyond his limits and used up all 100 percent that he discovers a new well of strength to draw on. This is why martial artists push themselves to the limit, beyond their limits, to total exhaustion. Then you can see the water in your cup. This is the meaning of *zanshin*.

Taking Responsibility

One way in which I have changed because of my budo experience is a gradual reluctance to blame misfortune on others. Life has its ups and downs. Relationships go bad, you lose your job, and your dog dies. When bad things happen, people have a tendency to look for something, or someone, to blame. It could be as simple as believing that they are down on their luck. Why blame luck? Hindsight often shows us that culpability lies within. With a little humble introspection, it soon becomes evident that failure is almost always the result of a lack of *zanshin*. *Zanshin* is the ethic of taking responsibility for your own destiny.

Of course, we may be adversely affected by another's incompetence in an organization setting. In that case, we may be inclined to shake our heads in despair and profess our own innocence. Another option would be simply to respond to the new circumstances, without complaining, and say, "Okay, what's our next option?" People who understand *zanshin* rarely get bogged down by saying, "Woe is me." They are forever looking at what they can do next or moving on if need be. Everybody has their moments, especially me, when we lose sight and fall back to the blame game default setting. *Zanshin*, when I have a fleeting moment of clarity, is my "safe word." It knocks the sense back into me and allows me to see things objectively again.

You never know whom you will face next in kendo. All *kendoka* have a few preferred techniques, but you cannot be sure whether they will be effective against any given adversary. What to do? You can stick to your same old familiar pattern in a bout, but if it is clearly not working, flogging a dead horse is not usually the best strategy for victory. If one kind of technique is ineffectual, try another. If that doesn't work, what about this combination? What if that does not go according to plan? Change your timing and cadence. Coax your opponent into dropping his guard. Plan B, plan C, Plan D ... Open mind, flexibility, preparedness to adapt, confidence to overcome any hindrance. This is literally a test of your ability to think on your feet. In this way, kendo trains you to embrace adversity and take great joy in trampling it underfoot.

I may find opponent "A" easy to beat. "A" might have no problem defeating opponent "B." But I might have trouble tackling "B." It is not that opponent "B" is superior in skill; it is because my kendo is still undeveloped. Opponents come in a wide variety of personalities, body types, and levels of experience. Knowing how to deal with them is not only a matter of rational analysis. It is something we learn through practice and more practice. If we practice hard, day in and day out, knowing what to do becomes second nature. If we fail to learn from each new experience (opponent), we never grow stronger. Win or lose, succeed or fail, the martial artist always pays attention and painstakingly searches for ways to clear each hurdle in the dojo, and in life. That is *zanshin*.

Stress Less

It dawned on me that when I lose kendo matches, it is not because of inferior ability but because I am internally weak. This is the first step in purging yourself of weakness and developing strengths. Kendo is very good at exposing your foibles, warts and all, whether you like it or not. At work, and in personal relationships, we are confronted with various inconvenient truths that invoke a sense of insecurity. Most avoid looking too deeply into our own personal Pandora's box. Over the years, I have learned to approach life's little problems as I would a kendo match. In situations where I used to become highly agitated, I now recall the importance of *zanshin*. Whether I get angry and succumb to my emotions is entirely up to me. I am not always successful, of course, but my life has much less stress as a result.

At the Naginata World Championship in 2011, I lost in the final, and had to settle for second place. My opponent's blade did not touch me, but the judges decided that his technique was good enough. I lost because of that "point." If the same kind of erroneous judgment occurred in a soccer match, there would be hell to pay. There was nothing I could do. All I could think was, "I see. The referees based their decision on my opponent's movement. I put myself in a position where I was unable to show them otherwise." I accepted my loss and learned from it. I had no time to dwell on the past and what might have been. It was time to move on. Losing is an important learning opportunity. This is also *zanshin* at work.

Although I certainly cannot claim to have eliminated stress from my life, it is easier to manage. The ability to remain composed in the throes of chaos, paying close attention to everyone around you is an outstandingly germane legacy of samurai culture. Like samurai, we must take responsibility for our own actions and be accepting of the consequences. *Zanshin* is an important concept that connects old Bushido philosophy to modern budo ideology and, hence, self-perfection through the vehicle of Japanese martial arts.

Budo and Self-Perfection

I do not claim to understand all there is to know about *zanshin*! Far from it. I was in my mid-thirties before I got an inkling of its depth.

Practicing *naginata* at the Shubukan Dojo in 1990.

I had already spent nearly twenty years in the dojo. I had little epiphanies along the way, but it did not click until I had accumulated a modicum of life experience with which to associate it.

The dictates of kendo are strict. One must always maintain sangfroid and never be rude to opponents. The *kendoka* comes to internalize these rules over time. The attitude for respectful interaction with others manifest in your behavior and actions. It does not happen overnight but is an incremental process requiring some "tough love" from your instructors and a willingness to face your demons—and plenty of blood, sweat, and tears.

If a high-school student pumps his fist during a kendo match and loses a hard-earned point because of a fleeting moment of uncontrolled excitement, the normal reaction would be to take pity. The truth is, whether the student realizes it or not, he may have just learned a valuable lesson that will last his whole life. Of course, just because someone does kendo does not mean he or she becomes a model human being, a paragon of morality. There is no doubt in my mind, however, that budo teachings contains time-honored insights into the human condition, and *zanshin* is of the essence.

If *zanshin* is applied in one's personal philosophy for navigating life in contemporary society, I believe the possibilities are limitless. Everything I know about life I reaffirm through kendo. Japanese martial arts are a transcendental path through which one can grow. At least for me now, kendo is my skeletal structure, on which the flesh of life clings. It is my religion, and *zanshin* is its constitutional doctrine.

CHAPTER 2

Koyo-gunkan and the Ideal Leader

Wisdom Forged in the Furnace of War

Myriad books, old and new, convey various aspects of Bushido. The old ones were written for the edification of samurai and contain recommendations on how to live a life bereft of shame. The new ones reinterpret these ideas to make them relevant for people in contemporary society. Directives in the old books are often obscure or even reprehensible to modern sensibilities without some contextual understanding; but some tenets are still germane even without much adaptation. Among the old books, one that stands out for me is *Koyo-gunkan*, an early seventeenth-century text about the exploits of Takeda Shingen (1521–73) and his son, Katsuyori (1546–82). They were powerful daimyo of Kai (Koshu) province during the Sengoku period (1467–1568). A very different time, for sure, but the book is replete with astute observations on human character and the shortcomings of those in power, counterbalanced with detailed advice on how to avoid destructive pitfalls.

Because of its characteristic preoccupation with questions of death, Bushido is sometimes thought of as a kind of archaic existentialist fundamentalism. A search for veiled meaning in samurai chronicles, however, indicates that balance and moderation were crucial cornerstones of the samurai way of life. *Koyo-gunkan* makes this abundantly clear. In this chapter, I examine some of the main ideas espoused in *Koyo-gunkan* to see how it defines the ideal leader in accordance with the exigencies of the age.

Kosaka Danjo Masanobu (1527–78) was an experienced combatant who prospered in the service of both Shingen and Katsuyori. He is credited with writing the text, although authorship is very much a matter of conjecture. Because he was a direct retainer of Shingen and Katsuyori, his firsthand observations are undoubtedly an important feature of the twenty volumes and fifty-nine chapters that make up the *Koyo-gunkan*. The writings were compiled by Obata Kagenori, a renowned military scholar and teacher of Takeda military studies in 1621, but he probably wrote the lion's share.

Kosaka was born into a farming family but entered the service of Shingen at the age of sixteen, eventually rising up the ranks to become one of the legendary "twenty-four generals" in the Takeda army. The formidable Takedas were obliterated in Katsuyori's generation by Oda Nobunaga and his allies, and the book was crafted as an expression of Kosaka's grief at their downfall.

Koyo-gunkan became a popular read when it first appeared but is riddled with historical errors through one-eyed adulation of Takeda glory. As such, it has not been held in particularly high regard as a trustworthy source by scholars, even though it abounds with hints on what made samurai of the Sengoku period tick. *Koyo-gunkan*'s pages are peppered with military teachings from the Chinese classics. Shingen's battle standard slogan, *fu-rin-ka-zan* (as swift as wind, as silent as forest, as fierce as fire, as unshakable as mountain), was appropriated from the ancient book of military tactics by Sun Tzu known as *The Art of War*.

Avoiding Overkill

The overarching theme of *Koyo-gunkan* is the avoidance of excess. Shingen advocated that winning six or seven battles out of ten is sufficient. Accordingly, a victory rate of eighty percent is dangerous, while a rate of 90–100 percent would mean an unacceptable number of needless casualties. In other words, ten out of ten wins equates to a terrible rate of attrition of his men, meaning that the battles may be won, but the war would be lost because of it. A victory rate of 60–70 percent is the best way to minimize the squandering of fighting power and ensure there is always strength in reserve. As for the rest, the best policy is simply to mitigate damage as much as possible and sometimes retreat even if a win is imminent. A general had to know which clashes were all-or-nothing and which skirmishes should be avoided as pointless. They had to pick their battles to be effective.

> Lord Shingen said, "In preparing for battle, those under forty years old should strive for victory; those over forty should aim to avoid defeat." When he was around twenty, he engaged with inferior enemies with enough force to avoid defeat but did not crush them with excessive force. This is even more relevant with regard to powerful enemies. It behooves the general to think hard on the matters at hand to devise strategies and plans of action, apply enough pressure

to squeeze the enemy, but have the foresight and patience to work toward overall victory in the future.

It was about pacing oneself. Winning by too large a margin is risky, and points to the necessity of balance in everything. Shingen's philosophy of winning is both rational and flexible and demonstrates a strong degree of pragmatism.

Samurai Raison d'être

The samurai ruled Japan for over seven centuries thanks to their political acumen and skill at arms. When the world became more peaceful beginning in the Edo period, the samurai were hamstrung, with no opportunities to put their fighting skills to work. Modern sensibilities would welcome peace, but in a subculture premised on accruing honor through exploits in war, political and social amity sparked some confounding issues.

How could they justify their existence? They were not farmers, so they did not grow things. They were not artisans, so they did not make things. They were not merchants, so they did not sell things. Their identity was tied up in their ability to fight—killing things—which was not a problem when a lot of killing needed to be done. In an epoch with little to no major conflict, samurai, who occupied the top echelon of society, had to find a new raison d'être. Such was the identity conundrum samurai faced at the onset of the Edo period and what stimulated the creation of a new kind of early-modern samurai ethos.

The *Koyo-gunkan* became a kind of Bible to samurai who beheld warriors of the good old days—when men were real men, and swords were kept well oiled in blood—with a sense of nostalgia and envy. The great generals of yesteryear, former clan enemies included, were regarded with great deference. *Koyo-gunkan* influenced subsequent books addressing the warrior peacetime philosophy thanks to the prominence of Obata's illustrious disciples, such as Yamaga Soko and Daidoji Yuzan. *Koyo-gunkan* was often quoted in their works as a source that best communicated the quintessence of Bushido. The samurai of the day had fallen into grousing that their existence was superfluous in peacetime. They had lost their mojo, and it was fast becoming a world of pretense in which lily-livered "yes men" prevailed. *Koyo-gunkan* was a reference that reminded samurai that traditional values of pragmatism were just as valid in times of peace as they were in war.

Of course, countless other treatises discussed military matters and offered the samurai cause to think and refocus their identity while preserving the essence of being warriors. Because of the "brush and sword in accord" tradition that had taken hold in the Muromachi period, elite samurai took to writing memoirs and admonishments to not-yet-born descendants. They combined family and military history with matter-of-fact advice designed to guide them in not making asses of themselves in the highly judgmental warrior community of honor. These books would later become points of reference for Edo-period samurai.

Four Doomed Lords

One of the more interesting chapters in *Koyo-gunkan* discusses four kinds of lords whose character traits would ultimately lead to the destruction of their clan. It describes their shortcomings, and the inevitable process of events that would typically unfold under their hegemony. The narrative then goes on to contrast these flawed individuals with the kinds of outstanding men who should be top dog.

The four condemned types are the "Foolish General," the "Cowardly General," the "Overly Clever General," and the "Excessively Strong General." First, the Foolish General. Common sense dictates that an imprudent leader will never be effective. The author of *Koyo-gunkan* offered a detailed analysis of what he meant by "foolish." Such a leader was spoiled, liked to cavort and have a good time, and found it hard to be serious in the best of times. The foolish lord was obsessed with the genteel arts: Noh and Kyogen theater, poetry, flower viewing, moon viewing . . . Military arts, however, such as archery and swordsmanship, were not at the top of his to-do list.

Of course, he would be politically naive. Yes-men with their own agendas float to the top of his coterie, and truly loyal vassals, who care enough about the traditions and well-being of the clan to remonstrate with their lord, end up incurring his wrath. Seeing their service as futile, they abscond to greener pastures, leaving the "avaricious toadies" to rule the roost—the end being, predictably, clan annihilation. Imagawa Ujizane (1538–1615), the tenth patriarch of the Imagawa clan, a dedicated aficionado of poetry and *kemari* (an ancient Japanese version of hacky sack), and who turned on the Takedas by foolishly enacting a salt embargo, was the poor stooge singled out for this ignoble assessment.

If leaders are incapable of evaluating the abilities and emotions of their subordinates, *Koyo-gunkan* warns, star vassals will leave, and only sycophants will remain. That is how organizations fall apart.

An example of a Foolish General in today's world might be an incompetent CEO, who inherits the mantle of power from the company founder (daddy), only to squander the company's assets in casinos, impulsive investments, priceless works of art, and houses of ill repute.

Next is the Cowardly General. Being paranoid, a Cowardly General suspects everyone and trusts no one. The Cowardly General purges his organization men with whom he does not get along and keeps only those who never question his authority. Before long, his underlings are all conspiring to undermine one another, and through treachery and betrayal may even take over the fiefdom or cause its disintegration.

No good can come of a Cowardly General. In the world of the samurai, cowardice led to fleeing the battlefield out of fear of death—the greatest shame for samurai whose highest value was honor based on valor. Alas for the Cowardly General, his disposition would attract only the dregs of samurai society—those whose chief concern was their own profit and gain. Unable to see their dastardly designs, the Cowardly General's paranoia acts as a noose around his own neck as he tolerates those currying favor and spurns those who are critical. As when pearls are cast before swine, the Cowardly General is unable to discern the true talents of his men.

Cowardly Generals will be cool, detached, and most likely very cruel. They are not stupid by any means. In fact, they may have genius-like qualities but are devoid of compassion—a subject I return to later.

Koyo-gunkan spotlights many such men, most notably Uesugi Norimasa (1523–79), a pathetically ineffectual daimyo. Through a succession of disastrous campaigns, he was forced into becoming the adoptive father of his former vassal, Nagao Kagetora, and handing the reins of power to him. Kagetora was none other than Takeda Shingen's greatest and most respected rival, Uesugi Kenshin. (Samurai changed their names several times over their lifetime.) Many of history's dictators, it could be said, fall into this category: Hitler, Stalin, Kim Jong Il.

Caustically Clever

Anyone can see why Foolish and Cowardly Generals are doomed. The Overly Clever General, and the Excessively Strong General, however, are more problematic. The Overly Clever General, as the designation suggests, is certainly not dumb. He is, if anything, too smart for his own good. How can a leader ever be too intelligent, you may ask? What could possibly be wrong with a leader who has a brain? Being exceedingly canny, he knows—to the point of arrogance—that he can rely on his own abilities to get things done. Shrewd and confident in his calculations, his words and actions may not always be consistent, but his unbridled pride makes him easily depressed and withdrawn when things do not go his way.

He will come across as aloof and seem to know everything. The truth is, his "superior intellect" makes him essentially blind to the ways of the world. Convinced of his own cleverness, he does not listen to his advisors and commits many needless blunders because of it. Driven by his own selfishness, he fails to appreciate the value of those toiling under him. Both the work he assigns to his subordinates and the compensation he gives them for their efforts are grossly misgauged. Capable men become despondent and abscond from his service, leaving only schemers who have no compunction about acts of betrayal if it serves their needs.

Because he is standoffish, he cannot solidify a meaningful bond with his men. He fails to hear or see what is really going on, and few can generate a genuine sense of loyalty to him. Stuck in a vicious cycle of suspicion, talented men are driven away by fear of becoming embroiled in a coup d'état even if their consciences tell them to stay. *Koyo-gunkan* points to Takeda Yoshinobu (1538–67) as a guilty example here. Yoshinobu was Shingen's son. He rebelled against his father and was imprisoned for being a terribly naughty clever boy. His grisly fate? Slitting his belly open to atone.

Intelligence and a healthy state of mind are two different things. Some people may be smart but still lack mental toughness or common sense. They may be swimming in knowledge but deficient in basic human skills and values, often failing to grasp the bigger picture. According to *Koyo-gunkan*'s analysis, he who is too smart will have a nervous disposition and will surely lack emotional stability. This description perhaps applies to feeble intelligentsia—the ones in their ivory towers who are summarily lined up against the wall when revolution comes.

The Burden of Strength

The last of our four types is the Excessively Strong General. Surely strength is a virtue in a military commander. How could a leader be "too strong"? *Koyo-gunkan* has a lot to say on this subject as it was directed at none other than Shingen's successor, Katsuyori.

> The Excessively Strong General lets nothing pass him by. Unable to show restraint, responding with force is his go-to move. His men are of a similar disposition, and many will die needlessly in the smallest of skirmishes because they do not hold back. Out of 100 excellent samurai, at least twenty of various ranks will die needlessly because of this.

The Excessively Strong General is mentally tough, able to think quickly on his feet, and eloquent in speech. At first glance, he is the leader we all want to follow. Ironically, his greatest weakness is his hatred of weakness. He thinks weakness is a flaw to be expunged with no mercy. Lords who pride themselves on strength and lack familiarity with failure all believe that their way is the right way. They have no patience for others with a more cautious approach. Prudent advisors will refrain from speaking their minds. They know that their leader will not listen, so they offer only pro forma counsel and will eventually avoid saying things that really need to be said. Excellent men in positions to proffer apposite advice and remonstrance will seek other places to serve because of their frustration, only to be replaced by those who mimic their almighty leader. Ultimately, no one listens to anyone else, and, although esteemed as the alpha male, the Excessively Strong General will end up a lonely figure.

A common Achilles's heel in these flawed leaders is their inability to appreciate the talents of their men. One of *Koyo-gunkan*'s important messages is that nobody can accomplish much of worth on his own.

It is incumbent on those perched higher up on the ladder to set an example for those below. The leader must recognize the talents and abilities of his men and delegate missions accordingly. This was simply a matter of survival. When a leader is "too strong," his hubris and self-righteousness will cause the organization to crumble under his very nose. "Their excess of self-confidence makes them no good for anything. ... Their main obsession is to outdo their own fathers."

In Kosaka Danjo's summation, Katsuyori would stop at nothing to surpass Shingen, as is not uncommon with many young men under pressure to fill the gigantic shoes of their fathers. Before he could fill his father's shoes, Katsuyori shot himself in the foot by being "too strong" and is widely blamed for extinguishing the bright flame of the Takeda clan. The truth was far more complicated. Katsuyori was an outstanding general in his own right. Otherwise, Shingen would never have chosen him as his successor. Katsuyori was every bit as talented as his father, but, alas, he tried to overdo it. He should have had more confidence in his own ability, and Katsuyori's advisors, Kosaka believed, failed in their grave responsibility to make sure he kept on the right path.

Balance

The tone of *Koyo-gunkan* is unabashed in its reverence of Shingen as the ideal warrior. Shingen was both smart and strong. What was the difference between him and other lords who were too "smart" or "clever"? The crux of the matter is the word "too." One constant in *Koyo-gunkan* is the assertion that balance is important and that extremes are to be avoided at all costs. Strong is good, but "too strong" is counterproductive. The book is chock full of examples on the maintenance of equilibrium in an array of situations. From military strategy, everyday living, to the character of a military leader, these examples often take the form of admonitions: "Taken to excess, this is what will happen …"

Kosaka concedes that even bad leaders have good points; but it is the excess that makes them toxic. "The leader who lacks balance is a failure. The outstanding general should be strong when needed, yield if need be, charismatic when necessary, and merciful when compassion is called for." The important thing is the ability to change and adapt to the situation and have enough wriggle room to be spontaneous. Changing times require a stalwart philosophy tempered by an open mind.

Operating between two extremes is not a simple matter of muddling through in mediocrity. It is about dead reckoning your way through life; going with the flow and tailwinds when possible, and taking some inevitable deviation from your course into account. Early eighteenth-century books on Bushido, such as *Hagakure* and *Budo-shoshinshu*, seem overly rigid in their advice, but closer inspection reveals a common theme of maintaining balance remained a chief consideration well into the era of peace, albeit expressed it in different ways. Why is balance so important? This question cuts to the heart of Bushido.

The Ingenuous Mind

The ideal leader, as described in *Koyo-gunkan*, is associated with a few key words: forbearance, discernment, consideration, compassion, and combined cultivation of the cultural and military arts. Again, it is all about balance, the ability to control emotion, and patience to bear the unbearable (*kannin*). "Discernment" (*funbetsu*) is the prudence to differentiate good from bad, right from wrong. A leader who takes any one trait to excess is described as "lacking in discernment," a potentially fatal shortcoming. Such a person is unable to accurately assess the true intentions of those who serve him. Disenchanted men who might well have been intensely loyal to their lord end up leaving. Only fools and horses remain. "Consideration" (*shinso*) refers to empathy—the ability to imagine the thoughts and feelings of others. For samurai, this kind of thinking is closely tied to the imperatives of honesty, sincerity, and lacking a fear of death.

A renowned scholar of samurai ethics, Sagara Toru, referred to the sum of these ideals as the "ingenuous" (*arinomama*) attitude—a virtuous temperament mentioned throughout *Koyo-gunkan*. Sagara argues that samurai who respect things and themselves "just as they are" will never lie or make excuses. They stand proudly before others "comfortable in their own skin." Part of being ingenuous is to take full responsibility for both word and deed and never blaming others for mishaps.

Ingenuousness was requisite for all levels of samurai, from the generals down to the rank-and-file. As analyzed in *Koyo-gunkan*, a good vassal is willing to speak his mind frankly and to make his word his bond. Lords were morally accountable for keeping an open ear to forthright opinions tendered by subordinates for the sake of the traditions and future prosperity of the clan. *Koyo-gunkan* informs us that samurai who were prepared to die at any time set no store whatsoever in "profit and loss" like the money-grubbing merchants. For warriors, the imperative attribute was to be unafraid of death and to use this mind-set as collateral for the sincerity of his word.

Still, *Koyo-gunkan* can be confusing because of its contradictory turns of phrase in the text. For example, the Koshu Laws—reproduced in *Koyo-gunkan*—admonishes people to "speak little" of men of higher rank, implying that one should keep one's opinions to oneself. At the same time, it proclaims the importance for those of higher status to listen intently to the opinions of minions and make sound judgments based on that information. Prepared to die if that is their fate, vassals should shoot from the hip and continue to offer counsel and information to Shingen and others they regarded as leaders, if they truly believe it is for the good of the clan. This is precisely the essence of ingenuousness.

The leader may view unsolicited remonstrance as a nuisance, even a slight on his personal honor, in which case the messenger will slice open his own gut to redress his "impudence." If that happens, then so be it. The vassal accepts his own demise if his lord so commands as he is already prepared to die. "As you are" then becomes "as you were" but was considered a worthy death if it was presented as a frank and honest assessment of the status quo, neither taunting nor toadying. "Even a hint of embellishment will make the truth seem false." Ostentatious shows of pretense were abhorred as this ran counter to the essence of "as you are."

The ideal leader listens to his supporter's counsel in the grace that it is given. "I see. Is that so? Got it. I will take that into consideration." The lord's deportment is what enables samurai to live as true samurai. On the surface, communication between master and servant tended to be in one direction—downward—but in the *Koyo-gunkan* ideal, subordinates could state their views without concealment. In other words, the quality of the vassal depended on the quality of the leader. What makes the "ingenuous" mentality possible, and indeed useful, is a balanced philosophy of leadership that takes everything into account.

It Takes Two to Tango

Related to the idea of balance is a fascinating clause, Article 17, in the Koshu Laws. It states that in a quarrel, irrespective of who started it, both sides will be apportioned equal blame. If two samurai get into a fight, as they were wont to do, then punishment will be meted out to both, regardless of who is right or and who is wrong. It was a harsh law to dissuade samurai from "losing their rag" and starting what could easily escalate into a violent feud between families within the province and beyond. This could threaten the order, stability, and peace within the realm. For this reason alone, the rules called for harsh punishment for both antagonists involved in an altercation if only to prevent the conflict from spreading. Penalties included death by either dismemberment or ritual suicide.

The Takeda family was certainly not the only clan to adopt this code, but it was one of the first. Shingen's men were not thrilled by this restrictive measure designed to control their highly volatile sense of honor. Naito Shuri, a stalwart of the Takeda army and one of Shingen's most vocal advisors, was indignant.

"This is absolute nonsense, m'lord."
"Why do you say that?"

"Suppose some samurai insults me. If I must endure it without repaying the slight to my honor, then am no better than a useless coward? If both are to be blamed and punished for the insolence of one, then all will shy away from doing what's right. Who wants to be punished needlessly? Samurai will back away from any fracas, even if the stain on their honor brands them as a [scared] chicken for eternity. Do you really think that samurai who accept this as the norm will be of any use in battle?"

Naito was worried that this rule would make the Koshu samurai feeble and flabby and that the Takeda army would become a laughingstock of good-for-nothing asses, too scared to fight for what is right. His advice reflects the "ingenuous" samurai psyche in terms of what he was trying to say, and the fact that he had no qualms about calling it as he saw it. He was lauded as a truly loyal vassal of Shingen's, peerless in his resolve as a man who could walk the talk.

Shingen understood what Naito was saying. He understood, but he still concluded this rule was for the good of maintaining order in his province. He was between a rock and a hard place, as the following story shows.

If a Job's Worth Doing ...

Shingen proclaimed this law in 1547, when he was twenty-seven years old, and it was an actual fight that prompted it. A skirmish broke out between two samurai, Ako Zekisaemon and Terakawa Shiroemon. Terakawa grabbed Ako by the breastplate and knocked him to the ground. At the time, Terakawa was about forty, and Ako was fifty-six or fifty-seven. Ako had fallen to the ground and could not get up, but countered with a splendid kick. Terakawa fell backward and was knocked out cold. The spectators debated among themselves who had won the brouhaha.

When the incident was brought to Shingen's attention, he was furious.

> You call yourselves samurai? Why did neither of you draw your sword and cut the other down? Why or how the fight started is irrelevant. One side felt insulted and sought redress. Why did you not fight to the bitter end instead of bickering like children? Where is the honor in that? When two samurai fight, they must be prepared to draw blades, to draw blood, and to draw their last breath. How would this pathetic display look to samurai of neighboring provinces?

Shingen dragged Ako and Terakawa by their noses and shamed them publicly. Then he banished them. Ultimately, both men were later beheaded for their troubles. Such a contradiction! Or so it would seem. His law that incriminated both sides in a fight was designed to quell fighting among his men. At the same time, it was an admonition that if you get into a scrap, at least have the guts to see it through. Either way, one or both is going to die, so it might as well be for protecting your honor rather than via the executioner's sword after the fact.

Samurai were compelled to defend their honor, even at the cost of their lives. Honor was worth more than his life, as it was not only individual honor in question but that of his ancestors and descendants, and of the clan he served. A trivial dustup between two unknown samurai led to a raging and ongoing debate that highlighted the dichotomies and contradictions samurai faced as they tried to be "ingenuous." It resulted in a law that still confounded samurai centuries later during the Edo period.

Shingen's Koshu Laws remained influential long after the fall of the clan. The Tokugawa shogunate promulgated similar rules to prevent unsanctioned outbreaks of violence. Honor revenge was possible but required official approval from one's own feudal lord, and endorsement from magistrates in the shogunate. Without that restraint, as peaceful as Edo-period Japan was, it could have quickly descended into chaos. Edo Japan was infused with an undercurrent of tension, and samurai were a volatile bunch always spoiling for a fight. A simple misunderstanding over something as inconsequential as an innocuous clash of scabbards in the street could easily get out of hand, threatening the very order of society.

As a case in point, one bloody incident of vengeance in the Genroku era—the infamous forty-seven ronin affair (1701)—was a sensational event that divided opinion throughout the country. The meticulously planned assassination of Lord Kira by the aggrieved retainers of Lord Asano was, and still is, celebrated as a righteous, beautiful display of selfless loyalty in tune with samurai custom. Then again, they brazenly and knowingly broke the law with their unsanctioned assassination—so were they therefore not just common criminals? Public opinion was divided, and their violent actions no doubt incited more than a few bar fights. I return to this incident later.

Three ronin samurai attack the entrance to Kira's home. (*Juichidanme* by Utagawa Kuniyasu [Between 1815 and 1818] Retrieved from the Library of Congress, <www.loc.gov/item/2009615198/>)

Forbearance

Shingen's kerfuffle prevention edict comes with a curious "out clause": Fighting for any reason whatsoever shall be punished. That was clear. However, if party A picks a fight with party B, and party B does not react, B shall not be punished. This is related to one of *Koyo-gunkan*'s keywords, "forbearance" (*kannin*). In other words, the proper response to antagonism is patience, tolerance, and not taking the bait. Samurai were bred to defend their names with whatever force was necessary.

That attitude was fundamental, but strength demonstrated through forbearance was also important. Essentially, a demonstration of forbearance was idealized as being more valid in the pursuit of honor than resorting to knee-jerk violence. *Kannin* was the samurai "chill pill." The problem was knowing when to take it, as forbearance was sometimes a hard pill to swallow.

Non-response was as good as death, especially if the aggressor had drawn his sword! In this case, the only possible conclusion was that you were damned if you do and damned if you don't. Die in the flap, or die later on, when punished. If anything, it made samurai more hell bent on going for the jugular when the going got tough. Maybe, just maybe, this was Shingen's intention all along. It was hidden messages/enigmas such as this that tantalized generations of samurai in the Edo period and why *Koyo-gunkan* was on any serious samurai's bookshelf.

Greater Strength Equals Greater Compassion

Another central ideal espoused in *Koyo-gunkan*, "compassion," may seem counter-intuitive considering the inherent pugnacious tendencies discussed above. Then again, it fits perfectly with the notion of balance. The Sengoku period was brutal. It was about killing, usurping, treachery, one-upmanship, headhunting, and a lot of general destruction. No matter how tenacious and unyielding the samurai was in the throes of combat, he was not the real deal without an equal portion of compassion. No compassion meant that the all-important balance was missing. Yin is incomplete without yang, and, for a samurai, compassion was as important as military skills.

Shingen was a devout man, who reputedly never killed women

or children, unlike some of his more vicious contemporaries (Oda Nobunaga). His enemies respected him for this. After all, war is war, and collateral damage was just one of those things. Not so for Shingen, who believed that compassion was an essential string on the warrior's bow. The samurai plied his trade in war; carnage was his calling. He had to be strong, even vicious, as a weak or cowardly warrior was of no use on the battlefield. Shingen believed, however, that a warrior's strength was augmented by a kind heart. Without it, a samurai was no better than a random murderer, an ogre.

Shingen was revered as a powerful general long after his death. Edo period samurai held his teachings and wisdom in high regard. Whether this evaluation was accurate is really of no consequence, as he was seen to embody the perfect combination of strength and compassion—the stuff of legends in samurai society. If anything, I suspect that the samurai probably had a far more vivid appreciation of the beauty of life and the weight of one's words and actions than we moderns can claim.

Compassion was viewed as the mark of a true man. One saying goes: "A strong samurai often sheds tears." Even for mighty warriors, an awareness of the fleeting nature of existence was the *quidditas* of his emotional makeup, aesthetics, and compassion. The superlative samurai, as they saw themselves, was both coldhearted and tenderhearted at the same time, but never halfhearted.

The daimyo of Echigo province during the Sengoku period was Uesugi Kenshin, the warrior mentioned above. He believed that samurai who were determined to survive were the ones more likely to be killed. Fear of death in a warrior would, paradoxically, be his undoing. That is why a warrior trained his mind and body to be resigned to such a fate. To prepare one's mind for death, the argument goes, one must first jettison all that he holds dear. To let go of something precious requires immense determination and grit and is a sign of true strength. The stronger the warrior, the more intense his compassion. One of the most famous quotes from Shingen is: "The people are my army, the people are my stone walls, the people are my moats, compassion is my ally, enmity is my enemy." Given the times, there was plenty of enmity to go around, but kindness was hailed as proof of strength and a resignation to death to see the majesty of life itself.

Power and Pacifism

By today's moral sensibilities, the ostensible cruelty, stone-faced disregard for life, and atrocities committed by samurai do not deserve glorification. "Valorous butchers" they may have been, but they were also acutely aware of the sinfulness of their violent métier. As the old expression *bushi no nasake* (samurai-like compassion) suggests, showing mercy and compassion amid the hell was affirmation of his humanity, his contrition, his melancholy, his strength, and his empathy for other warriors in the madness. It reminds me of the mandatory sense of contrition in the notion of *zanshin*.

Another dualistic relationship that emerges in samurai society is the connection between strength and pacifism. Taking another's life was a matter of survival, and mortal combat was the apogee of the samurai profession. But rare is the person who can kill another and escape the burden of guilt. One of the vestiges of samurai wisdom still taught in the martial arts today is that the ability to take life teaches the warrior the nobility of peace. During the Sengoku period, several notable swordsmen, such as Kamiizumi Ise-no-Kami, reached an impasse after years of killing their way through life. He and others propounded the idea that the stronger the warrior, the more likely it is that he would become a proponent of peace.

It is easy to think of the samurai as exterminators who treated life with disdain and discarded it without a second thought. Old samurai treatises indicate that nothing could be further from the truth. Of course, in Japan as in any region in the world at any given time, there will always be psychopaths who take sadistic pleasure in slaughter. In a world where anyone could be killed at any moment, the ranks of the samurai had their fair share of homicidal maniacs. This would explain why the theme of compassion is featured so prominently in much of the samurai literature throughout the ages. It was an ideal that distinguished the best from the rest, and to which all were meant to aspire.

Kendo Kata and Compassion

The concept of compassion remains an important consideration in the martial arts. The Nihon Kendo Kata comprise a set of ten predetermined forms studied in modern kendo. They were created in 1912 for the purpose of teaching a standardized version of kendo in Japanese schools. Students mainly study competitive full-contact fencing with bamboo swords and protective armor. The kata were developed to supplement the sporting version and teach aspects of swordsmanship, such as etiquette, gaze, stance, posture, breathing, principles of using a real sword, appropriate distancing from the opponent, footwork, and technique.

A man whom I consider one of the greatest kendo masters of the postwar era, the late Inoue Yoshihiko, explained to me the less obvious meaning behind the forms. It was his belief that one only need to understand the first three of the ten kata to grasp the essence of kendo. The Nihon Kendo Kata are performed by two people: the *uchidachi*—usually the senior adept, whose job it is to teach the junior *shidachi*. The *uchidachi* is the "aggressor," in the kata. He strikes first but will be counterattacked and defeated each time.

In the first kata, both sides assume the *jodan* stance, in which the sword is held in an imposing position overhead. Both swordsmen advance three bold steps simultaneously to reach the danger zone, where one more step forward by either side will reach the target. The *uchidachi* takes an almighty swipe at the *shidachi*'s head. The *shidachi* steps back to dodge the blow and then steps back in with a counter cut to the *uchidachi*'s head. Obviously, the blade is stopped a hair's breadth from the flesh, but the encounter figuratively ends with the *uchidachi* being decisively cleft in twain. Any blow to the head with a sword would be decisive. The *shidachi* wins, the *uchidachi* is dead.

In the second kata, both assume the middle stance (*chudan*) with swords held in front of the body, tips pointing at the other's throat. Three steps in, and the *uchidachi* unleashes an attack to the *shidachi*'s right wrist. The *shidachi* steps back to dodge the cut and then immediately counters by stepping back in and cutting the *uchidachi*'s right wrist instead. The *uchidachi*'s hand is now metaphorically severed, and it is the *shidachi*'s victory once again. Why doesn't the *shidachi* opt to strike the *uchidachi*'s head and kill him outright? The opportunity was certainly there.

What about the third kata? Both start with their swords in the lower *gedan* stance, with tips pointing to the ground. Three steps in, the swords are raised slowly together. When the tension reaches a crescendo, the *uchidachi* thrusts his blade at the *shidachi*'s solar plexus. The *shidachi* fends off the thrust by stepping back and returns the favor with an immediate counterthrust. The *uchidachi* retreats, but the *shidachi* keeps the pressure on and follows, pushing him back further with the point of his blade raised to touch the perspiration between his eyebrows in a display of penetrating *zanshin*. The *uchidachi* concedes, but theoretically not a drop of blood has been spilled.

Although he is defeated, the kata is not over at this point; the moment the sword is elevated to the spot between the *uchidachi*'s eyes is a fateful moment of do or die. The *shidachi* is nonverbally communicating to the *uchidachi* that his life can be snuffed out in a nanosecond. Both the *uchidachi* and the *shidachi* reflect on the poignancy of this predicament and come to an unspoken mutual understanding that it is better to return without the coup de grâce. The *shidachi*: "I have no interest in killing you if I don't have to." The *uchidachi*: "I have no wish to die if I don't have to." Both: "Life is good, let's get on with living ... Phew."

In the course of the kata, the *uchidachi* has allegorically sacrificed himself as the teacher to guide the *shidachi* incrementally to a realization of *bushi no nasake* (mercy of the samurai). The first set is a decisive victory. In the second, there is a victory but not a fatality. In the third, there is neither victory nor defeat. In Master Inoue's words, to fight while also having refined humanistic sensibilities groomed through study of the classics, grace in manners and etiquette, and a compassionate disposition. In other words, cultivating competence in both the military and the cultural arts was concomitant with cultivating humanity.

Through the craft of war, samurai accumulated knowledge and power and were inordinately proficient at adapting to changing times. While maintaining a semblance of consistency in their thinking and behavior, they successfully continued to rule Japan for over 250 years after the pandemonium of civil war ended. Perhaps the ultimate example of their adaptability was demonstrated by the events leading up to and after the Meiji Restoration of 1868, when the shogunate was replaced by a new imperial government. Seeing the urgency of catching up with the Western powers, the samurai cast aside their customary feudal system of warrior rule and remodeled Japan into a modern nation-state, to the detriment of their own social status. It was a kind of "social seppuku" for the greater good. The dynamism behind this decisive action was, unquestionably, the samurai norm of holding both military and cultural arts in the highest regard. They were smart enough to know they had to move on.

Lessons from *Koyo-gunkan*

Among the many documents written about military studies in medieval and early-modern Japan, *Koyo-gunkan* held a revered position and popularity as a guide to many samurai, a testament to the prestige of the Takeda clan.

Of course, as a product of its times, *Koyo-gunkan* contains passages that are fictional or simply mistaken. The image of Shingen has been somewhat deified, and some may disagree with his reputation of greatness. The book contains many contradictions and paradoxes. Vassals are urged to be prudent when speaking to their lord but, at the same time, to advise them forthrightly, even at the cost of their own lives. Samurai are told not to fight but also to "defend their honor to the death." They are instructed to sharpen their killing skills but also not to kill. They are expected to uphold both strength and compassion.

Is it a matter of picking and choosing? Playing things by ear? Being flexible? A text such as this is open to a wide range of interpretations. *Koyo-gunkan* aside, Bushido is a way of thinking that is rife with incongruities and open to a wide range of interpretations. As we see in Chapter 3, my own personal understanding of *Hagakure*, for example, has changed tremendously over the past twenty years. At the very least, however, if you wish to understand how medieval samurai lived, you can find no better primary source than *Koyo-gunkan*.

Although there is always the unsolvable problem of context, *Koyo-gunkan* contains an essential, immutable humanism that transcends time, from the Sengoku period to the Edo period and even to the present. For warriors who navigated the precipice between life and death, these teachings represented the balance needed to exist in the most human way possible in borrowed time.

What do we, as global citizens in the modern age, need to survive in the most human way possible? What are the most important things in life? *Koyo-gunkan* and other classic books on military lore provide us with numerous invaluable hints, if we know how to interpret them in the right way.

Shingen had some words of advice for his followers on how to live life to the fullest. He said to one of his attendants, "There is one way for all men, regardless of rank, to save themselves. What do you think it is?" He thought about the question for a while and replied, "Having discretion at all times?" Shingen turned his head in disapproval. "No. Rather than doing the things you want to, throwing yourself into tasks that you don't want to is the best way to appreciate that you are alive. This is how you live life to the fullest." I sort of get what he means, especially when I have to get up at 5:00 am in the freezing cold every morning to go to midwinter training! As they say, "if it doesn't kill you, it's gotta be good for you."

CHAPTER 3

Dead Ready to Live: *Hagakure* and *Budo-shoshinshu*

Edo Period Samurai: Chalk and Cheese

As Japan fought its way through the tumultuous Sengoku period in the late fifteenth and sixteenth centuries, warrior ethics reflected a world of extreme violence. Death was not an abstract ideal; it was very real. With the establishment of the Tokugawa shogunate early in the seventeenth century, the country was finally ushered into an era of cautious peace under the shadow of more than a century and a half of pandemonium. The code of the samurai, predicated on day-to-day intimacy with death, was no longer in step with the times. Men of war were now called upon to fill administrative positions in the organs of provincial and central government.

Although not as prosperous as affluent townsmen taking advantage of the flourishing economy, those with the birthright of samurai status occupied the top echelon of society over the farmers, artisans, and merchants. Nevertheless, justification for warrior authority in Pax Tokugawa started to be called into question, not by their social inferiors, but by the samurai themselves. A new kind of "Edo Bushido" was the order of the day—an ideology that valued the customs and spirit of yesteryear's warriors, but was more conducive to the paradigms of Tokugawa amity. The warrior mind and his credo needed refocusing.

So-called Edo-period Bushido evolved with considerable regional variations. For the sake of convenience, scholars in Japan broadly divide the early-modern warrior honor code into two kinds. The first was provincial samurai psyche represented by classic treatises such as *Hagakure*. It demanded uncompromising fealty to the domain lord and typically was unabashedly region-centric. Depending on how far away the province was located from Edo, it could be tinged with seditious anti-shogunate sentiment. I refer to it as hardcore "bullheaded Bushido."

The other kind of Bushido, represented by texts such as *Budoshoshinshu*, was a fusion of Confucian and military studies and emphasized appropriate law-abiding conduct for all samurai, rather than members of a given clan. The duties of the samurai were spelled out unambiguously in the form of "how to" manuals. Although death remained a primary consideration, maintenance of social order following Confucian precepts was the overarching theme. I call this soft-core "balmy (=temperate) Bushido."

Eminent scholar on samurai ethics and thought, Sagara Toru, loosely categorized these two modes of samurai dogma as "*Hagakure*-esque Bushido" and "Confucian Bushido." They make a remarkable study of contrasts but also had many aspects in common. First, at their core was an acceptance of and preparedness for death. Always central to the warrior ethos, death was to become even more idealized during the Edo period as the reality and memory of war faded.

One of the best-known passages in *Hagakure* states, "The Way of the warrior is to be found in dying." This sentence is often sadly misconstrued. It was even commandeered as a catchphrase by the militarist propaganda machine in the 1930s and 1940s. If we take the axiom at face value, it appears that seeking to sacrifice one's life for a cause is the ultimate expression of being a warrior. This may be true, but it is far more complex than this one-dimensional exegesis would suggest. As with so many classic treatises on Bushido, reading between the lines of the standard hard-nosed exhortations reveals a profound view of our precarious human existence. Paradoxically, this infamous homily is an affirmation of life, a message to samurai to make their ephemeral existence as luminous as possible for the infinitesimally brief time they occupy this world.

What can we moderns learn from this? In this chapter, I discuss the samurai's ostensibly fatalistic attitude toward death and contrast differing perceptions of this spiritual ideal in *Hagakure* and *Budo-shoshinshu*.

Fool's Paradise

The Japanese today often draw comparisons between themselves and samurai of the Edo period, but not always as a positive affirmation of their identity. For example, *heiwa-boke* is a ubiquitous term in Japan that means something along the lines of "peace stupor." In other words, those whose lives are so far removed from hardship and conflict that they no longer experience a real sense of crisis or urgency. It points to a miasma of apathy in the younger generation. They live in a fool's paradise and have degenerated into lethargic, apolitical, selfish reprobates concerned only with frivolity and appearance. This epitomizes many criticisms aimed at samurai around the mid-Edo period, as well as the postwar baby-boomers and subsequent generations who know very little about the dark years of the 1930s and 1940s. An old kendo teacher and Imperial Japanese Army veteran relayed to me his disdain of the young "peace idiots" of today: "They don't know how lucky they are. Problem is, they don't really give a damn either."

Pax Tokugawa was problematic in that the samurai had to redefine their existence and find new ways to embrace the quintessential warrior ideal of having one's deportment revolve around concerns of life and death. A samurai was expected to keep up an appearance of vigilance and wait in anticipation for an opportunity to repay his stipend and obligations with his "life." At the same time, however, the Tokugawa shogunate demanded that samurai avoid conflict and maintain the status quo so as not to threaten social stability. The shogunate outwardly urged military preparedness, but preferred habitually hot-blooded samurai to remain in a peace stupor for the sake of harmony in the realm.

Raised in a subculture predicated on bellicose ideas about honor, even the most trivial spat could rapidly escalate into a death match threatening public order. There was always a need, and an expectation, to be prepared for emergencies, but there was also considerable pressure on samurai to contain their explosive wartime temperament. Allowing citizens to go about their daily activities peaceably is the mandate of all sovereigns. The last thing anybody wants is extremist rebels without a cause threatening to wreak havoc because they are unfulfilled.

How then, was the samurai to assuage his hunger for honor? It required a dexterous, but frustratingly contradictory balancing act:

being militarily prepared and adhering unquestioningly to the stoic covenants of his code of honor, but stopping short of enacting his deepest desires and fantasies to confirm his courage in the cauldron of conflict. The currency of honor had to be earned in different ways: from gallantry in battle, it became commensurate with his ability and dedication to duty and service. This required more discipline than ever before, but peacetime ennui was becoming an all too common affliction.

Vexation at the waning spirit of the samurai is the rationale behind *Hagakure*. Those who soaked for too long in the Jacuzzi of peace were in imminent danger of diluting the very source of what made them samurai. Samurai were forgetting the glorious legacy passed down to them by their valiant forefathers. It was this bequest that provided the foundation of his very being and permitted him to stand alone as a true man among men. *Hagakure* provided later generations of samurai in the Saga domain with lessons on their shared past and well-meaning albeit acrid advice pertaining to the protocols and mind-set of ideal deportment in their world of service.

Hagakure was written in the early eighteenth century. Yamamoto Jocho (1659–1719), a former retainer of the Saga domain (Nabeshima clan), orated his curmudgeon-like take on the world and reminiscences of historical events to his junior Saga colleague Tashiro Tsuramoto. Tsuramoto visited Jocho over the course of seven years at his little hermitage in the mountains of Saga and diligently recorded their discussions for posterity. It might not have been that way, for Jocho instructed Tsuramoto with a standard idiom of humility to "burn the text" once completed. Thankfully for us, he didn't take that ultimatum in the literal sense.

When Jocho's lord, Nabeshima Mitsushige, died in 1700, it was his professed intention to follow him to the netherworld as the greatest expression of loyalty a warrior could show in peacetime. This kind of ritual suicide by disembowelment (seppuku), known as *junshi* or *oibara,* had already been outlawed in the Saga domain (1661) and by a national decree issued by the shogunate (1663). Evidently, too many warriors were killing themselves on the passing of their lords through personal choice (or peer pressure) as their great adieu to the mundane world and a final display of their rectitude and loyalty. Denied this honor, Jocho chose to hang up his swords and take the tonsure, leaving clan service to live out his remaining years in a thatched hut. *Hagakure* is a memoir of lamentations by a loyal retainer thwarted in his desire to perform a suicidal swan song of stubborn fidelity.

Life was simpler in the good old days. Honor, the all-important currency of the samurai, was won on the battlefield through demonstrations of valor or death. Now, they could no longer stake their claim in the killing fields. They were even prohibited the right of a self-willed death as proof of their unflinching loyalty because of bureaucratic injunctions that spat in the face of their manhood. Jocho's eventual response to this Catch-22 was simple. Samurai were to throw themselves into the loyal service of their lord and domain and live each moment as if it was their last.

Live an Extra Day

Around a decade after *Hagakure* was completed, the military scholar Daidoji Yuzan (1639–1730) wrote *Budo-shoshinshu* (1725), a sort of self-help book to keep samurai on the straight and narrow. Yuzan's teachers, Yamaga Soko and Hojo Ujinaga, were celebrated scholars and strategists. Yuzan studied classics such as the *Analects of Confucius* and the works of Mencius and deliberated on how these philosophies could best be applied to new-age samurai conduct. Soko's teachings on the "warrior's creed" (*bukyo*) were a tour de force in the process of codifying a new peacetime ethos. Yuzan's *Budo-shoshinshu* was a continuation and further refinement of Soko's work. Incidentally, both men were students of Obata Kagenori, the compiler of *Koyo-gunkan*.

Representative of "balmy Bushido," *Budo-shoshinshu* does not see eye to eye with the bullheaded *Hagakure* in some key areas. That is not to say that Yuzan had ever heard of *Hagakure*. He most certainly had not, as *Hagakure* did not circulate outside Saga until the early 1900s. Yuzan embraced the Confucian-inspired view that samurai should live as "superior men" in the world, while seeking to preserve peace for the greater good.

> Above all, know that a samurai's body and life are not his. To fulfill his duty of service, the samurai must be prepared to do whatever his lord requires. To this end, the samurai one must treasure his life, avoid intemperance in eating, drinking, and indulging his carnal desires. Strive to live even one day longer so that you can serve your lord to the very end. Believing that dying from illness in your bed is not fitting for a samurai, and instead engaging in meaningless altercations or silly arguments resulting in the death of friends

or risking injury to oneself, is the height of disloyalty and misconduct, and to be avoided at all costs.

Dying quietly in one's bed, Yuzan believed, was a far more constructive way for a samurai to end his life. Thus, striving to "live even one day longer" was the finest way to demonstrate one's devotion. It was also a warning by Yuzan about how quickly things can get out of hand if you let your guard down. This attests to an undercurrent of tension that existed in big centers such as Edo—a melting pot for samurai from rival clans all over the country.

Budo-shoshinshu preaches the importance of family life and harmonious personal relationships, alongside studying the classics and the upkeep of military skills. Its rubric is detailed and specific. Yuzan reaffirms warriors' identity and social responsibilities and, in the process, prescribes a code of conduct and etiquette for daily life. This was in stark contrast to the impetuous vignettes found in *Hagakure*. It was a gentler rendition of the warrior's way, tailored to the new breed of narcissistic metro-samurai. *Hagakure* criticized this brand of Bushido as a wimpy, debauched mind-set detached from the true calling of the warrior. He despised how his countrymen (i.e., from Saga) would come back from their missions in Kyoto and Edo emulating in speech and manner the decadence of cosmopolite samurai. Such assertions were provocative and meant to be so, but Jocho was certainly not the only proudly bucolic samurai in the Edo period who embraced such a reproachful view.

The two books were the chalk and cheese of Bushido—one was politically correct, and the other most certainly was not! Nevertheless, the fact that such disparity in opinion regarding the samurai ideal coexisted is telling for several reasons. First, when people speak of Bushido, as they frequently do in Japan, exactly what kind of Bushido are they referring to? It is all too often lumped into one big ball of clay without contextual considerations of region and time. To put it another way, baseball, kendo, playing video games (e-sport), and synchronized swimming are all categorized as sports, but they are very different entities in form and manner.

Second, the samurai were becoming snobs and/or slobs, a far cry from the image of superhuman beacons of staunch masculinity and righteousness that we moderns like to entertain. Third, that time and ours share interesting similarities. People in Japan are continually disturbed by an apparent moral decline in the spoiled X, Y, and Z generations, the fading of Japan's vitality as a nation, and the *heiwa-boke* parasitical "peace idiots" who, in their soft fool's paradise, contribute nothing of substance to society.

Given this perceived state of affairs plaguing postwar Japan, a revival of Bushido is often trumpeted as a timely remedy, just as the samurai looked to the past to guide their way into the future. Moreover, at that time, like now, a lot of confusion as to what Bushido actually was, what it is, and what it should be. What was the quintessence—the everlasting pervasive universal truth—that myriad forms and interpretations of Bushido had in common? Reading between the lines of these texts is the only way to fit the pieces together, but an ability to contextualize the insanity and keep an open mind is imperative.

Banned Book vs. Bandied Book

Hagakure and *Budo-shoshinshu* also had different histories in terms of dissemination and readership. *Hagakure* was a kind of manifesto recorded by a member of the Nabeshima clan for fellow clansmen. Jocho was particularly critical of the escalation of "balmy Bushido," seeing it as a desecration of the true warrior mind and traditions—much as how people nowadays decry the negative influences of globalization on the integrity of indigenous cultures. Although Jocho was aware that his contemporaries could not be facsimiles of samurai a century earlier, he was adamant that the cultural and spiritual chain linking them to their Nabeshima forebears should never be broken. In this sense, *Hagakure* has been referred to as an expression of Nabeshima nationalism.

Although three centuries have elapsed since its completion, *Hagakure* was by no means a widely known text in Japan. It was a controversial book even within the Saga domain because of its unflattering appraisals of many illustrious families and retainers in the service of the Nabeshima lords. Furthermore, Jocho made no secret of his antipathy toward the shogunate. *Hagakure* was censored and was never utilized as a textbook at the Nabeshima clan school for children of warrior families, the Kodokan. People in Saga knew that the book existed, but it was not talked about in polite conversation. Jocho's rambling sermons contained too many inconvenient truths.

The first time *Hagakure* became known outside Saga was March 1906, when a local elementary school teacher compiled a selection of aphorisms for publication. It was not until 1935 that the entire text was published in Kurihara Arano's *Hagakure shinzui* (Essence of *Hagakure*), followed by the meticulously annotated *Hagakure kochu* (*Hagakure* collection) in 1940. *Hagakure* had emerged from the mists of obscurity just in time to be "press ganged" into becoming a symbol of the militarist agenda—a stigma that it still has not entirely shaken off.

Budo-shoshinshu, by contrast, was a homogeneous introduction to Bushido for middle- to lower-level samurai and was also widely read by commoners. It was a bestseller in its day, but surprisingly few people know about it now. In fact, after publishing a paper about it a couple years ago, I surprisingly received an e-mail from Yuzan's great-great-great grandson thanking me for awakening him to the book's immense sociohistorical value. Apparently, his grandfather talked about it when he was too young to care, and it had never occurred to him just how prominent his illustrious ancestor was in the evolutionary process of Bushido.

Hagakure is in many ways a mordant, sometimes humorous, but very perceptive account of the degeneration of warrior values. Although not overtly seditious in tone, it did expound a version of samurai fundamentalism and could easily be interpreted as championing unbridled violence as the answer to everything. It all depends on how you want to read it. *Budo-shoshinshu* portrays the ideal samurai as upstanding members of society, loyal to authority, devoted to their parents, fair in their dealings with others, and engaged in the perpetual pursuit of knowledge. The book styles a moral direction for samurai that was as innocuous as it was concise. It is easy to see why "peace idiot" samurai might prefer a straightforward "paint by numbers" manual akin to the self-help books of today, rather than a cold, hard assault on the senses that a book such as *Hagakure* delivered. Both books, however, constitute a fascinating hole-in-the-wall view of the trials and tribulations of samurai life.

Death for a Long Healthy Life

Despite clear differences in overall tone and intended audience, central to both was the way they address questions of mortality. From its very first pages, *Budo-shoshinshu* emphasizes a perennial awareness of death as the samurai's most important mental task.

> The instant a samurai takes his chopsticks to pluck lumps of rice cake from porridge on New Year's Day, until the very last day of the year, he must keep death, above all other things, firmly in his mind. Constantly thinking about death, a samurai simultaneously treads the path of loyalty to his lord, and filial piety to his parents. No matter what ill fortune or calamity may befall him, he will prevail and live a long and healthy life with this mind-set. What's more, he will become a better person for it, imbued with many virtuous traits.

Yuzan goes on to note that failure to contemplate death will invite unforeseen catastrophe and cause the samurai inadvertently to sully the name of his lord.

> Be they of high rank or low, a man who puts death out of his mind will lead an unhealthy life of overeating, drunkenness, and lechery. Accordingly, he will suffer illnesses of the spleen and kidneys, and die unexpectedly young. Even if he lives, he

will subsist as a good-for-nothing burden who is consistently under the weather. He who is ever mindful of death will appear younger than he really is, and will remain hale and hearty. He will eat properly, be judicious in his intake of booze, and distance himself from illicit encounters. He keeps in good health because of his moderation. This is the secret to enjoying a life that is long and robust.

We see here that Yuzan's motivation for maintaining an "awareness of death" is to foster attributes such as forbearance, modesty, balance, and a realization that the body and mind are terribly fragile. Mindfulness of one's mortality, he argues, is required of a samurai lest he squander his life in frivolity and excess, cutting short the time and usefulness of his tenure in service. The name of the game was to "live long and prosper," not to blow the gift of life—needed to repay your social obligations to serve—in a fleeting lapse of reason.

He promoted the cultivation of the military and cultural arts as the key to self-improvement for both elite and lower-ranked samurai, and stressed the importance of harmony and teamwork in the workplace. One gets the distinct impression through reading his text that samurai society was a proverbial house of cards. Mindfulness of death was knitted into all aspects of Yuzan's instruction because carelessness would have far-reaching consequences. One fool's moment of belligerence could ruin it for all. He was clearly a rational and judicious man.

Take the Hard Road

How did Jocho view death? What did Jocho mean when he wrote,

"The way of the warrior is to be found in dying"? *Hagakure* states plainly that when a samurai is faced with two choices, he should boldly jump into the fire.

> If one is faced with two options of life or death, simply settle for death. It is not an especially difficult choice; just go forth and meet it confidently. To declare that dying without aiming for the right purpose is nothing more than a wasted "dog's death" is the timid and shallow way of urban warriors. Whenever faced with the choice of life and death, there is no need to try and achieve one's aims. Human beings prefer life. As such, it is a natural tendency to apply logic to justify one's proclivity to stay alive. If you miss the mark and live to tell the tale, then you are a coward. This is perilous. If you make a mistake and die in the process, you may be thought of as crazy, but it will not bring shame. This is the mind-set of one who firmly lives by the martial Way. Rehearse your death every morning and night. Only when you constantly live as though already a corpse will you be able to find freedom in the martial Way and fulfill your duties without fault throughout your life.

Jocho poses the question that when a samurai faces an extreme situation, should he choose a course of action in which death is less likely, or not? A samurai who elects the safe option, he argues, may survive but will live the rest of his life in shame as the "coward who ran away." Shame was the samurai's kryptonite. A blight on his personal honor also meant a stain on his family line—past, present, and future. The stain of shame could be bleached out of the family underwear only through ritual suicide, the good old gut cut. The safer option for self-preservation, according to Jocho's logic, turns out in fact to be the more precarious.

If, however, the samurai opts for the perilous road instead, his impending downfall might be derided as a meaningless death, but it is a course of action befitting a samurai. It is a death with honor. And, given his single-minded resolve devoid of trepidation for the bloody consequences, he actually has a higher chance of survival and may be able to solve the problem once and for all. It is a win-win outcome. The choice was between dying in shame and dying with honor. The answer is a no-brainer for Jocho, as circumventing shame was paramount in the sardonic samurai community of honor. It could be argued, in fact, that the avoidance of shame was a greater concern than that of achieving honor.

Letting Go

There were only two choices. The only possible outcome for hesitation is the tar pit of shame. Don't think too deeply about every little thing, Jocho advises, as this is an indication that a samurai has not done his mental homework. "Preparedness" means that, when the time comes, and you never know when that will be, you can act appropriately and spontaneously without wasting time deliberating. His message was: Be prepared. "There is no time to be sluggish or fall behind. A true man of service leaps unflinchingly to his rendezvous with death, come what may." Jocho recounts the following interesting story to illustrate what he means by "manly decisions" to "put your balls on the line."

> Once, a group of ten blind monks was walking through the mountains. As they passed the top of a cliff, their legs began to tremble, and although they took extreme care, they were overcome by fear. The leader staggered and then fell off the edge. The rest all cried, "Oh what a terrible end!" They were unable to take a step further. The blind monk who had fallen off the cliff yelled up from below: "Do not be frightened. Falling was not so bad. I am now quite unperturbed. I worried about what would happen if I fell, and was somewhat apprehensive. But now I am very calm. If you want to put your minds at ease, just do it. Quickly fall and get it over with."

The original Japanese text uses the term *sutemi* for "fall," which literally means "discarding the body." It is a common word in the parlance of kendo and the other martial arts. It teaches the magnitude of sacrificing yourself fully in the attack—expunging any tentativeness and striking with total conviction the instant opportunity knocks. This, of course, is easier said than done. Until people "let go" and take the plunge, they are hamstrung by their anxiety about the consequences. What is needed to win in kendo and, by Jocho's summation, to win in life, is the conviction, courage, and confidence engendered by *sutemi*, and to be unconcerned by whatever you *imagine* might befall you.

When the moment is right, there is no time to dilly-dally over all the "what ifs." Such details should have already been considered in your off time. A samurai must be decisive and throw himself wholeheartedly into the fray. It may appear reckless; but is it really, if mind and body are prepared well in advance to deal with any situation?

Another keyword associated with this mind-set is *shini-gurui*, a term I translate as "death frenzy." With the usual angst that people have about discussions of death, this phrase may seem somewhat alarming. It is another one of *Hagakure*'s concepts that is inevitably misconstrued or at least open for interpretation. Think of it here as the mental attitude that underpins *sutemi*.

> Bushido is to enter a "death frenzy." Even dozens of men cannot kill a samurai [if he is] in a frenzied state, already determined to die. Lord Naoshige said, "One cannot accomplish great exploits in a normal frame of mind. Just become insane and seek death head-on. In the Way of the warrior, contemplating matters too deeply will cause you to fall behind others. Don't think of loyalty or filial piety, just enter a frenzy ready to perish in the fray. Loyalty and filial piety will manifest as a matter of course with the death frenzy mind."

Figuratively speaking, "death frenzy" does not mean you are determined to self-destruct or kill. It means drawing on a latent internal power so great that it elevates you to a different plane of being, and enables you to accomplish whatever it is that you need to do. It means being able to face danger directly and acting with the total conviction of *sutemi* without hesitating. To achieve this state, you must be resigned to the possibility that you may very well perish in the process. Therefore, being prepared to die is, paradoxically, the best way to make the most of life. And, as Jocho repeatedly stresses, if you are going to die anyway (as we all eventually will), it is better to die in a blaze of glory. That was proof of a bona fide samurai and a life that meant something.

The Forty-Seven Losers?

Hagakure is an avowal of purity and sincerity in action and "living to death" with one's entire body and soul. Jocho proffers a virulent critique in the stirring tale of the "forty-seven ronin." This celebrated historical incident has been dramatized in all forms of media through the ages. A New Year's break would not be complete without a mandatory "forty-seven ronin" (*Chushingura*) movie on TV. The problem with the forty-seven masterless samurais' quest for revenge on the villain who besmirched the honor of their lord, Asano, was that they spent two long years formulating their plan. This is what *Hagakure* says on the matter:

> The ronin of the Asano clan were culpable for not immediately committing seppuku at the Sengakuji Temple [after the night raid on Lord Kira's mansion]. Moreover, it took too long after their master had met his demise to exact revenge. What if their intended victim, Lord Kira, had died of illness in the interim? It would have been a disgrace. Urbanite warriors are clever at finding ways of being showered in praise.

This print shows a scene during the attack on Kira's home by the forty-seven ronin, with the samurai chasing Kira's guards into the house. (*Juichidanme - act eleven of the Chushingura - assault on Kira Yoshinaka's home - pursuing the guards* [Between 1800 and 1850] Retrieved from the Library of Congress, <www.loc.gov/item/2009615293/)

The passage prior to this says:

> A samurai disgraced himself by not fighting back in a quarrel. To retaliate entails just frenetically throwing yourself at your adversary with the intention of being cut down. Being killed this way brings no shame. Thinking about how to win may result in missing the optimal timing to act. Or, being outnumbered, some men postpone reprisal to gather reinforcements, and eventually talk of calling the attack off altogether. Even if there are a thousand enemies in waiting, a warrior must have the grit to charge forth and cut through one after another. This can be unexpectedly successful.

The epithet "herbivore men" is trendy in Japan to label a new generation of males whose behavior conflicts with traditional models of masculinity. They are panned as having forsaken their "manliness." In 2010, 70 percent of men in their thirties who responded to a survey considered themselves "herbivores," characterized by an unwillingness to become romantically attached and an aversion to any kind of conflict. Indeed, Jocho's venom was directed at the samurai herbivores of his day. It is this kind of social commentary that makes *Hagakure* so fascinating and strangely relevant even now.

The *Hagakure* Hero

Hagakure celebrates calamities as opportunities. In a flood, "The more water there is, the higher the boat rises." Jocho asserts that it is not enough merely to remain calm in a catastrophe. "When challenged by adversity, charge ahead with courage and jubilation. This is rising to a higher level." Furthermore, "A competent man, or one engrossed in a pursuit he enjoys, will relish the challenge of surmounting difficulties. There is a huge difference between these men and those who feel as though they are drowning when the going gets tough."

When all bets are off, the ideal samurai is the *kusemono*, a word that now means "rascal," "rogue," or "slippery customer." To modern Japanese, it has mostly negative connotations, but not so in *Hagakure*. Far from it: Jocho uses the designation to define a samurai with strong beliefs and convictions. He might have a strange habit or two, but he is a man capable of acting decisively, when he is most needed. I translate *kusemono* in the *Hagakure* context as "hero." Jocho's father, Jin'uemon, once said,

> "Exceptional warriors [*kusemono*] are dependable men. Dependable men are exceptional warriors. I know this through considerable experience. Dependable men can be relied upon to keep away when things are going well, but will come to your aid without fail when you are in need." In other words, the ideal samurai "hero" has, on the reverse side of his cold hard martial ability, a most thoughtful, compassionate and caring personality. "Without strength, you cannot survive. Without compassion, you don't deserve to survive."

Hagakure also speaks of the intuitive nature of the ideal samurai in terms of his "powers of observation." He can perceive the subtle beauty in things that would normally be overlooked. Jocho recounts the story of a Nabeshima lord who was trimming his nails. The lord ordered a lowly servant to get rid of the nail clippings, but the servant noticed that one was missing. The lord had hidden it to see how he would react. The servant was not fooled and said, "One has gone astray. I cannot possibly dispose of them until I find it." The lord was satisfied that his servant was indeed observant. The message here is not about the complexities of personal grooming but that a samurai must cultivate keen powers of observation and never miss a beat. This is connected to the warrior's aesthetic sensibilities, and his ability to interpret the world empathetically.

Stop Clinging to Life

Hagakure's urging to be resigned to death is a core concept in Zen Buddhism. Yagyu Munenori, an early Edo-period samurai who wrote the classic and highly influential martial art discourse *Heiho-kadensho*, incorporated many Zen ideals into his teachings. He was presented with an essay on Zen by his mentor, Takuan Soho (1573–1645). The title of the essay is "Fudochi-shinmyoroku" (The Miracle of Immovable Wisdom), and Munenori quotes Takuan verbatim in several sections of his own book. In Takuan's essay, there is an interesting section titled "The Instant Response of Spark and Stone."

> There is a phenomenon called the "instant response of spark and stone." The instant you strike a flint, a spark is generated with no pause between the clash and the resulting light. This means that there should be no interval for which the mind

can become attached to something during the course execution. This is not simply a matter of performing that action as swiftly as you can. The crux is that the mind must never become attached, not even to speed. Thinking about rapid execution means that the mind is being diverted, and this provides an opportunity for the enemy. If you act quickly with the express intention of doing so, your focus on speed means that your mind has been captured by it.

What does this mean in the context of swordsmanship? It is a warning not to be distracted by the opponent's weapon. Focusing on the movement of the enemy's sword will cause your mind to be deceived. In the same way, Jocho was advocating that a samurai who becomes too attached to the idea of living will be terrified of death. A samurai who is afraid to die will be constrained, and neither his mind nor his body will function as it should. Conversely, we can say that the attitude of a resigned acceptance of death is the same as being liberated from unnecessary attachments. As a way of freeing himself from debilitating fear, the samurai had to realize that, as with the striking flint and the resulting spark, there is no pause between life and death. There is one, therefore there is the other.

> Once a samurai understands how life and death are inextricably linked, that the quality of one dictates the quality of the other, his heart will become unfettered, and he will be able to act as the situation requires. His actions will be more efficient, effective, and lucid. Train your minds to embody this ideal.

The same theme can be detected in the kata forms practiced in Japan's martial arts. Simply put, the kata in various budo traditions were designed for two purposes: to teach the adept how to kill, and how to die. The latter is one of the most salient features of Japanese budo but is often not picked up on. Martial arts of other cultures also have forms comparable to kata. Although some exceptions exist, Japanese kata generally require two people, as opposed to solo performances, as often seen in non-Japanese martial arts. Most Japanese kata also finish with a coup de grâce. That is, one of the two adepts is allegorically killed. By performing the "death role" in kata, the student inadvertently learns to overcome his fear of perishing in the fray.

In the kata of Japanese swordsmanship, the senior adept (*uchidachi*) in most cases performs the death role. In effect, he sacrifices himself to educate the junior adept (*shidachi*) in the appropriate striking opportunities. It is very much like playacting, and no one dies during kata training (at least not anymore), but I find it hard to recall many sports or athletic traditions other than budo in which participants actively engage in a "ritual of death," culminating in the metaphorical demise of one side, the compassionate teacher.

Self-Willed Death

Jocho points out that the value of a samurai's life will not become apparent until the instant of death. A wretched death was evidence of a wretched life. He did not mean this in the karmic sense but as a simple reference to the idea that you get out of life what you put into it. A samurai's honor was judged for posterity by the nature of his final moment, which is why the samurai cared so much about how it transpired. In other words, death is not the end of life but the completion of life. Death makes life a whole.

On the surface, death is the most obvious theme in *Hagakure*, to the extent that it can make for some terribly morbid reading. It has countless repugnant stories about torture, slaughter, and senseless violence. These stories, however, highlight the opposite of what samurai held dearest: quality of life. For this reason, the freakish custom of self-immolation that exemplifies the most mysterious facet of the samurai mind was his crowning glory. It was a statement of integrity and valor to put icing on the cake of life, not an escape from it.

As noted earlier, Edo-period samurai were faced with an existential crisis in peace and were at a loss for ways to demonstrate their worth. As a valid alternative to battlefield performance, an extreme method for a samurai to satisfy this obsession was to take his own life—slicing open his belly and revealing his soul to the world. Withstanding such unimaginable self-inflicted pain was commended as the utmost expression of courage. If done well with little squirming or grimacing, this death would carry honor confirming his pedigree and would extend to his descendants as well. Choosing the circumstances of one's death was the ultimate articulation of the samurai's independent will and tenacity.

Committing seppuku involved a variety of motivations. Some did it out of protest, for example, because their lord refused to accept his counsel. The vassal may decide that death would be the best way to express the solemnity of his feelings and finally get his point across. *Hagakure* advises that vassals always be prepared to forfeit their lives for their beliefs. Jocho even mentions some unscrupulous samurai who drew their short sword before their lord and began the performance of ritual suicide, imagining (hoping) that their lord would put a stop to things before they went too far. If that gamble did not pay off—too bad!

As an aside, the role of second (*kaishaku-nin*) was also considered a "great honor" that nobody really wanted. The *kaishaku-nin* was not an executioner per se but a man chosen to decapitate the seppuku-ee and put an end to his suffering after he had shown a sufficient degree of unflappable tolerance for the pain. Jocho was asked by his nephew, Sawabe Heizaemon, to perform the grisly task at his pending seppuku. Jocho replied to the sudden request with a letter.

> I empathize with your resolution and agree to perform this honorable task out of my respect for you. It was my first instinct to decline your request out of courtesy, but there is no time to excuse myself for any reason as the ceremony is to take place tomorrow, and so I humbly accept. I am greatly honored that you should choose me from among so many. Rest peacefully tonight in preparation for tomorrow.

To get it right took a bit of teamwork, especially if the condemned man loses his nerve and starts to writhe. "When this happens, wait for a while and encourage the man to compose himself. The deathblow will be clean if you can deliver it quickly during a moment of calm." The *kaishaku-nin* faced some risks if he did not get it right. "It is a difficult task not readily acknowledged, even if it is performed in an excellent fashion; but if the second slips up, it will generate a lifetime of embarrassment."

Ritual suicide became increasingly formalized during the Edo period. Some samurai used a fan, instead of a short sword and held it against their gut in a kind of make-believe. As soon as they touched the fan to their belly, their second would behead them. Such pro forma presentations of seppuku were acceptable in the community of honor, but only just. Reading countless anecdotes and admonitions on the samurai's matter-of-fact take on death in books such as *Hagakure* and *Budo-shoshinshu*, it is frighteningly clear how fundamental seppuku was to their way of life. Still, the fact that these admonitions were deemed necessary to record on paper also shows that samurai had succumb to an epidemic of lethargy. The penchant for older generations to criticize young people never changes.

Forgetting How to Die?

The toe-curling custom of ritual suicide through disembowelment is surely beyond our realm of understanding. It came in several different flavors: following one's liege lord into the next world; to take responsibility for some work-related error, or to fulfill an obligation of duty; to avoid allowing the enemy to take your life in battle. And then there was the ritual suicide of overwhelming regret at being unnoticed by one's lord. Some even committed seppuku to atone for their lord's transgressions so that he could save face! Indeed, with the number of seppuku incidents recorded in *Hagakure*, one wonders how any samurai were left in the Saga domain at all.

It was not only the men in samurai families who appreciated the importance of dying in a method appropriate to their station. Another story that beggars belief is the account of a samurai who got into an argument with three farmers and was beaten to a pulp. When he got home, his wife was not exactly sympathetic. "Have you forgotten how to die?" "Absolutely not!" he retorted. As they left the house together, she lectured him in the "Way of the warrior": "All men are destined to die at some stage. There are numerous ways, such as from illness, in battle, seppuku, or by being beheaded with hands tied behind your back; but to die dishonorably would be most regrettable." The samurai and his wife returned to where the three farmers were and waited for nightfall. They then attacked the three, killing two of them and wounding one. Mission accomplished, the samurai later committed ritual suicide, and his wife lived happily ever after.

What was the point of this story? The samurai should have killed the farmers when the fight erupted, or died in the process. After all, he was the one with the sword. His failure to do this was evidence that he had not completed his mental preparation to be ready for death at any time. He avoided disgrace by returning to the scene, finishing the business, and then killing himself. Jocho praised the wife who salvaged her husband's honor, and reminded him of the importance of being ready to expire honorably.

Sometimes, ritual suicide was "permitted" as a form of honorable punishment in lieu of being executed by someone else's hand like a common criminal. The following incident occurred in 1868, when political tensions and anti-foreign sentiment in Japan was at a peak. Some French sailors put ashore at Izumi, near Sakai Harbor in Osaka. As they were being questioned for what should have been a lawful disembarkation of the ship *Dupliex*, much was lost in translation, and they were attacked by members of the Tosa clan charged with security at the port. Eleven French sailors were slaughtered. France was naturally enraged and demanded that the government make reparations in the form of monetary compensation and the execution of those responsible. Twenty of the Tosa warriors were ordered to commit ritual suicide.

The clan members, burning with anger, complied. At the Myokokuji Temple in Sakai, the samurai slit their bellies open one by one. Some accounts of the event recorded that the samurai pulled out their own intestines and threw them in the general direction of the French witnesses seated nearby. The French observers were so horrified by the gore that they stopped the suicides after the eleventh. Nine lives were spared. One wonders how number twelve felt…

This came to be known as the Sakai Incident, and it was instrumental in making other countries aware of Japan's macabre custom, now commonly called hara-kiri in the West. The Sakai Incident later inspired well-known Japanese writers such as Mori Ogai, Ooka Shohei, and Shiba Ryotaro in their poplar dramatizations of the times.

The Hidden Well of Strength

Leaving the *Hagakure* for a moment, I would like to look at the career of Yamaoka Tesshu (1836–88), a man who attained the highest levels of accomplishment in swordsmanship, Zen, and calligraphy in the same era as the Sakai Incident. A celebrated servant first in the service of the shogunate and then the emperor, he founded his own school of swordsmanship, which he called the Itto Seiden Muto-ryu. Muto means "no sword" and refers to Tesshu's epiphany that the difference between the self and the sword, and the opponent, is illusory. All things are one and the same. Tesshu was praised by one of his notable contemporaries, Takamori Saigo (inspiration for the character Katsumoto in the film *The Last Samurai*), as "Someone who has no attachment to money, honor, or even his own life, and can be difficult to handle. That's precisely the sort of person who can accomplish great things in this world." And, indeed, he did.

Tesshu eventually died of stomach cancer. In his last years, he wrote tens of thousands of sheets of calligraphy. Before settling down to write, he would always take a sip of the ink, which is highly carcinogenic—I conjecture that this was the cause of his cancer. Why on earth would he drink ink? He wanted to understand the ink better, by becoming one with it. I learned this story from the late Terayama Tanchu, a scholar of Zen, calligraphy, and swordsmanship, who probably had the most extensive collection of Tesshu's writings in Japan. Like Tesshu, he liked to drink ink before putting brush to paper, and he, too, died of stomach cancer.

When I paid him a visit at his dojo in Tokyo, Tanchu showed me two examples of Tesshu's calligraphy. Both were renditions of the character 龍, pronounced *tatsu* or *ryu*, which means "dragon." One was written before Tesshu's self-proclaimed enlightenment on March 30, 1880, at the age of forty-five, and the other a year or two later. The first one might be described as powerful but somewhat rigid. I am by no means a connoisseur of art, and my handwriting is atrocious, but even to my untutored eye, the post-enlightenment piece was both yielding and effervescent. The ink looked as it had just been applied and might still be wet. Implausible as that might seem, it sparkled. The kanji even came across as a dragon about to fly off the paper.

Tanchu was delighted that I could infer the difference and was not simply trying to impress him. He explained that the second piece, completed after his enlightenment, reveals that Tesshu had gained acceptance of his mortality and an understanding of the transience of life, the universe, and everything. It was not just theory, but now was in his flesh and soul. In other words, as he was no longer attached to living, his spirit was free, and this showed in the ambiance of the second work of calligraphy. *Hoshin* (a free spirit) was a term used by the Zen monk Takuan Soho to indicate a state of mind in which one never has attachments or stops at a single point. It is a mind that forever wanders unimpeded. This was visible in Tesshu's calligraphy.

Many famous, somewhat apocryphal stories surround Yamaoka Tesshu. Over the years, fact has been blurred by fanciful accounts of his uncanny powers. For example, it is said that when he sat in Zen meditation, the energy emanating from his stationary mass, his free spirit, would cause rats to fall from the rafters! I suspect that this and many other similar stories should be taken with a grain of salt, but there is no doubt that the man was special in a cosmic kind of way.

Tesshu proclaimed that his acceptance of death and subsequent enlightenment was the culmination of austere training in swordsmanship. He studied many traditions before creating his Muto style. As a modern practitioner of kendo, I shudder when I think of the notorious training method he made his top students undergo if he thought they were "ready." In the demanding fencing marathon known as *tachikiri*, a single swordsman must fight hundreds of challengers, one after the other, without reprieve. Apart from a short break for lunch, the swordsman could not sit or remove his mask for a breather. From morning until night for days on end, he did nothing but fence. As those who went through the challenge said of their experience, it was so grueling that many passed out from fatigue even only after a few fights. Their legs would turn to jelly, and they would gasp for air. Not until they could gasp no more and gave up caring was the exercise said to have been effective.

Takano Sasaburo (1862–1950) was a monolithic figure in the development of modern kendo for educational purposes. Originally a police officer, he was a disciple of Tesshu's. Later in his career, he taught kendo at Tokyo Higher Normal School, a forerunner of today's University of Tsukuba. In a book marking the ninetieth anniversary of the police force, an account written by Takano describes a slightly watered-down version of *tachikiri* that he underwent at the police dojo as a young officer. It started at 6 pm and continued until 6 am the next day.

> The session took place at the Azumabashi Police Station in Tokyo, and "assistants" who were willing came from various stations to beat us to a pulp.... By midnight, my senses were completely numb. If we stood in the middle of the dojo in such a dazed state, the assistants would throw us down and hammer us. We would not pass the test if we did not hang on until the bitter end, but around 2:00 it became so excruciating that I really felt like quitting. ... With the growing light of dawn, we came to our senses again, and we sought out the individuals who were pounding us a short while ago and

gave them a taste of their own medicine. In the end, the three of us managed to survive until the end. Nonetheless, training from 6:00 until 6:00 was a truly miserable experience. We were permitted to eat three helpings of rice gruel over the twelve hours and visited the washroom three times. My body did not return to normal for a whole week. Although I snored loudly, my head did not sleep at all. All I could see in my dreams for the week ahead were images of fighting with a sword. Although crude to mention, my pee was bright red for a week as well because of the blood in my urine. Those were the toughest days of training in my life.

Tachikiri, as dished out by Tesshu, was not designed to develop techniques. It was an exercise in self-denial, squeezing the last drop of vitality from the mind and body. It destroys the ability to think, reducing the person to a state of "no self" with an empty mind. It is at that point that the mind, body, and technique become a consolidated "one." That is the very same liberation from the shackles of attachment and desire talked about in *Hagakure*.

Another of Tesshu's disciples wrote a diary about his *tachikiri* torment. Unlike Takano's, this version of *tachikiri* went on from morning to night for three days. After the first day, he was physically exhausted to the point that he could hardly walk. By the third day, he could not even muster the strength to drag himself from his futon. Somehow, with the help of his wife, he managed the excruciating crawl to the dojo.

As the bouts were a free-for-all for any challenger, one was never sure which opponent he would have to face. It was then that a notorious ruffian, the kind of sadistic bully who takes great pleasure in hurting his opponents, showed up. Upon seeing the arrival of this contemptible individual, the enervated disciple who by this stage could barely stand on his own two feet, suddenly jumped to attention and charged forth with inexplicable vigor to wipe the fiendish smirk off his would-be challenger's face. His body acted before his mind could tell him what to do. "Wait! That's enough!" Tesshu shouted. "You have passed the test." When one is in the proper, enlightened, liberated state of mind, the body responds reflexively no matter how exhausted it is.

Graceful Defeats Trump Disgraceful Wins

The demands and expectations placed on adherents of Bushido and their cultish fixation with death might appear to modern observers to be a perilous code of ethics best left in the past. I would agree on many counts. Still, I am a practitioner of kendo today, and the more experience I accrue slogging it out in the dojo, the more I understand the old samurai willingness to stake their lives on their actions. I am in no way advocating violence here; I am alluding to the sublime feeling of purity in action, the "never-say-die" attitude, and the nerve required to venture into the deepest reaches of the body and mind in search of fleeting moments of spiritual liberation.

I once asked Master Inoue Yoshihiko for some remedial instruction in kendo basics. I wanted to focus on doing the fundamentals properly and striking with absolute conviction (*sutemi*), renouncing the flesh and all attachments. To be strong in kendo, as in anything, you must first learn to "do ordinary things well." The fundamentals must be learned, relearned, and relearned again. You will never improve if you neglect the most mundane basics to focus on the flashy moves. Regardless of how gifted athletes are, peeling away the razzmatazz of their genius, you will always find that it is buoyed by profound mastery of the basics. If this is not the case, their skills will deteriorate with age. There is no such thing in kendo as retirement. We get better with age because our daily training consists of reviewing basic techniques, ad nauseam. The training exercises in which we typically engage, although not as draconian as *tachikiri*, are rigorous and intended to help us learn to "let go."

It might sound fanciful to the uninitiated, but there is an inextricable bond between kendo and samurai ideals of death. It permeates what we are taught and how we practice in the dojo. I would not say this if I thought that the point of kendo was simply to strike a designated target with the bamboo sword in reciprocal jousting for points. It is a journey without an end, one in which the *kendoka* has access to a treasure trove of profound wisdom that can guide us through life. It is a legacy of human knowledge that warrants preservation.

Observing the 2012 World Kendo Championship (WKC) finals in Novara, Italy, however, I came to a painful realization that kendo is starting to waver—or, at least, *kendoka* may be losing sight of what needs to be preserved as the lifeblood of this intangible cultural heritage. The problem came in the final bout, between Japan and South Korea. A Japanese contestant struck the South Korean with an admittedly light but decisive tap on the wrist, and that should have been the end of it. But the South Korean contestant rejected the judgment. He remained standing and refused to perform customary courtesies at the end of a match. It is a cardinal sin to express your disagreement with the referees' decision. A coach may lodge a protest to the court director, but this is extremely rare. No matter what the competitor thinks, if the referees are all in agreement, then that is the end of the story. The Japanese were quick to criticize the South Korean competitor's bald faced lack of manners.

From my perspective, though, some of the Japanese competitors in the final were equally discourteous. After scoring the first point, for example, one of the Japanese team members decided to play it safe, running away from any engagement to ensure that he would not lose. A win is a win, but from an ideal kendo perspective, it was a miserable bout of calculated, disappointingly cautious behavior. Many of the non-Japanese people in the audience thought that Japan's attitude was poor. It seemed as if the Japanese team was no longer intent on fighting "fair and square," in the spirit of true kendo.

The Japanese competitors, however, are stuck between a rock and a hard place. In spite of all the rhetoric about "correct kendo" and the "spirit of Bushido," Japanese team members know that if they lose, they will be lambasted after they go home. They compete under tremendous pressure to ensure, by hook or by crook, that they do not lose. In contrast to other more internationally established budo sports such as judo and karate, kendo is for the most part still dominated by Japan. Although the technical level around the world is improving by leaps and bounds, Japan and its formidable rival Korea are in a league of their own.

Because Japan is the country of origin of kendo, people get upset when a Japanese expert loses a match to a foreign exponent. In a sporting sense, it is an exciting upset. In awe of the almost superhuman Japanese kendo cyborgs, however, non-Japanese *kendoka* also harbor, perhaps unrealistically in some ways, a latent hope that they will still set the quintessential samurai example of beautiful, orthodox kendo, even if they end up losing a few matches along the way.

The final match undermined those expectations, not only for non-Japanese but also the many Japanese spectators in attendance. The Japanese fellow sitting next to me was crying. I asked him why. "I didn't come all this way to watch cowards fight. I'm ashamed." Cowards? Knowing many of the Japanese team members personally, and knowing the almost inhuman regime of training that they endure in preparation to represent their country, I thought this was rather harsh. If there is one thing that they are not, it is cowards. They are as hard as nails, all of them. Still, I do understand the sentiment from which such frustration emanates.

Back to *Hagakure* for an answer of sorts. Contests, martial or otherwise, between samurai have four levels of results: a graceful victory, a disgraceful victory, a graceful defeat, and a disgraceful defeat. The underlying premise in this aesthetic of competition is "how you win and how you lose are equivalent to how you live, and how you die." In the world of the samurai, a graceful, honorable defeat was considered far superior to a disgraceful, deceitful victory, even though losing meant death in mortal combat.

In that 2012 WKC final, Japan was victorious. It won on points, but in terms of the quality of kendo, it lost. It was a graceless victory. Some people might be okay with that. To each his own. To me and other cantankerous purists of Jocho's ilk, the means is not always justified by the result. It was a defilement of the attitude that makes kendo such a noble path to pursue for an entire lifetime. Just as the Olympic Games hardly represent the lofty Olympian ideals in the era of professional sports, kendo, too, is being reduced to a nationalistic point-scoring exercise with little evidence of its profound spiritual and philosophical continuum, which makes it so valuable to the human experience.

- Quality Victory
- Quality Defeat
- Devious Victory
- Devious Defeat

The four levels of results in any kind of contest according to samurai values.

From my perspective, it is incumbent on *kendoka* to fight gallantly, with grace, and from the get go. Then, even if one loses, at least it is a graceful loss. To me, that constitutes value more than what can be gleaned from a disgraceful win. Of course, the key to winning war is often deception and guile. Miyamoto Musashi's legendary tactics leading into his duel with Sasaki Kojiro were questionable from the perspective of "gentlemanship" or as a Way, but not war. That is why he was criticized by his contemporaries and later by himself. It is no exaggeration that the strong notion of honor in battle, whether in victory or defeat, has remained a core ideal in budo. *Hagakure* taught me how deep-rooted this value was in the samurai psyche and enabled me to identify it as one of the idiosyncratic values of budo. Then, as now, one of the most confounding problems in budo is the clash between pragmatism and idealism.

It also reminds me of the explanation of the Nihon Kendo Kata. It all fits. The execrable win-at-all-costs temperament seen so often at local and international kendo tournaments these days is essentially the same as the first kata. You need the skills to survive. It is kill or be killed. It is the first step in a long process of personal development. If people do not forget that winning is not the ultimate objective of the martial arts but, rather, a means to an end and not the end itself, then they will progress through the stages represented by kata numbers 2 and 3. These are infinitely more meaningful. If *kendoka* lose sight of this, in my view it will lead to a loss of immutable values.

It would be ideal if the superstars of the competitive circuit in kendo, the Japanese and Korean team members, could show the way. But they are young and have a job to do. They might not always fight in the spirit of kendo, but they are playing within the rules. So, maybe the rules of kendo should be revised instead. One-point matches, rather than the best out of three points, could be more conducive to the original ideas of kendo in making it an all-or-nothing affair, and more realistic in terms of being "sudden death."

The Ethics of Personal Responsibility

Hagakure is a discussion of resignation to and acceptance of death, but also of a passion for life that derives from that. What is meant by a passion for life? One motif that runs consistently through *Hagakure* is the idea of personal responsibility. The people who come in for the most virulent criticism in *Hagakure* are the self-centered sycophants. Feudal lords would surround themselves with advisors to assist in running their domain. One of Jocho's many gripes was that a fair proportion of them were old geezers who would spend their time criticizing others but rarely take responsibility themselves.

Jocho wanted to take responsibility for his lord's passing by committing ritual suicide, but was forbidden to do so. He chose to forsake the world instead, committing a kind of "social suicide." He was highly critical of other retainers in his lord's service who did not even entertain the idea. To Jocho, these men were reprehensible two-bit blowhards who knew nothing of true service. He names quite a few of them, which surely ruffled feathers.

Historically speaking, discourses on Bushido often proliferated in times of social change, both good and bad—in the Edo period, for example, when the samurai had to justify his existence; in the modern era, when Japan created a new national identity and then embarked on the slippery slope of militarism; and in the 1970s and 1980s, when Bushido was cited as one of the driving forces behind Japan's remarkable economic prosperity. Then, after the economic bubble burst, it was seen as a code of moral constants needed to revive Japanese confidence and pride and reverse the trend of moral decay.

Jocho's Bushido is about encouraging the samurai to aspire to become someone on whom others can rely when needed, people who are willing to sacrifice their own interests for others, people willing to do something for the world. What is needed is the good old *Hagakure* "*kusemono*." Embracing responsibility is what it takes to get things done. The "samurai" designation is used for male heroes of the sports world in Japan and others deemed gallant and manly. The image of the ideal person, the paragon of morality, that most Japanese people hold now is based on the samurai of the Edo period.

Representative of the samurai ideal is the notion of personal responsibility and a willingness to be accountable, even though it may cost them their life. Of course, more than a few samurai did not live in accordance with these ideals, hence the need for men such as Jocho to vent their spleen. It would surely have irritated the likes of Jocho and other samurai elites, however, that lowly commoners had ideas above their station and were adopting Bushido as their national mantra when Japan modernized. "Bourgeois Bushido?!" The insolence of it all! Nevertheless, if you ask a Japanese person "What does it mean to be Japanese?" one of the first words to escape their lips is "samurai."

In times of change, people in Japan show a tendency to look backward, rather than forward and try to avoid taking responsibility for problems that may eventuate in the future. This is by no means unique to Japan, but I am regularly dismayed by the reluctance of colleagues to take the bull by the horns on many issues simply because "it hasn't been done before." "If it goes belly up, who is going to take responsibility?"

Students at the university where I teach are an affable bunch but give new meaning to the word "apathetic." They do what they are told and without question. This is a worry itself; but a student who takes the *initiative* and does something of his or her own volition these days is as rare as an environmentalist in a whale restaurant. My students rarely demonstrate an inclination to take responsibility. I often tell them that they have two fundamental choices in life: they can accept the status quo forever and a day, or take responsibility for changing it and themselves for the good. If "the Way of the warrior is found in dying" means anything, it is to take responsibility in this way, for this reason. If you do not know what you should take responsibility for, just do something good for somebody else.

If You Like Sleeping, then Sleep

In the past, I did not have a very positive view of *Hagakure* because it is full of contradictions and became associated with a perverse nationalist agenda. It has earned a rather unfortunate reputation as an "evil book." Yukio Mishima, the renowned Japanese novelist, was a self-proclaimed adherent of *Hagakure* teachings. His ritual suicide through disembowelment in 1970, following a failed attempt to persuade Japanese Self-Defense Force members to participate in a coup d'état to restore imperial rule, was doubly symptomatic of a fanaticism to which I cannot relate.

Some English translations of *Hagakure* exist, but none are complete or contextualize the hidden messages in a meaningful way. I decided to undertake the task myself. In the process, I came to the realization that elements that, at first, seemed positively absurd actually had an internal logic and consistency. I became somewhat obsessed as I started seeing a clear method in the madness. Eventually, instead of feeling as if I was translating what was on the pages of my source text, I felt as though Jocho was lecturing me, and I was the playing the role of a blue-eyed Tashiro Tsuramoto as I recorded his dictations.

The ambiguity of the text confuses readers. One comes across conflicting advice from one page to the next. One moment Jocho is saying that the samurai must throw himself into service as if he were "already a corpse." Then he advises careful deliberation and a prudent choice of words. The discrepancies are easy to dispel with an understanding that samurai were not all equal. The hierarchy was a rigid one with many ranks. Accordingly, the ways in which each level of samurai was to serve would come with completely different expectations and method.

The lower-ranking samurai were called upon to figuratively, sometimes literally, give their lives for their lord. Higher-ranking samurai, however, were positioned to offer candid and timely advice. "The loyalty of counsel" required skills in diplomacy, selfless resolve, wisdom, and prudence. Honor was found in the act of offering judicious, yet discreet, counsel. This, too, was a precarious responsibility, as it might mean sacrificing one's life to take the blame for a lord's foolishness or to atone for angering him.

In other words, loyalty and devotion took different forms for the various ranks of samurai. The lower-ranking samurai showed his loyalty with his flesh. The higher-ranking ones with their minds. After we understand this, some of the "contradictions" in *Hagakure* no longer seem so incongruous. The common thread linking all ranks of samurai, however, was to serve with a single-minded pure will and intention, referred to throughout the pages of *Hagakure* as *ichinen*.

In any given passage of the book, we must look carefully to see which level of samurai is the intended audience for its message. In Chapter 2, I discussed the medieval law in which both sides involved in a fracas would be punished. The law was aimed at ronin, or lower-ranking samurai. A higher-ranking samurai would be treated differently. In this sense, it is not possible to talk about samurai as an undifferentiated group. Indeed, many of the famous books on the warrior's creed through the ages were directed toward those with a specific social standing. *Hagakure* was a mixture in this sense, which makes for considerable puzzlement.

Hagakure contains many descriptions of bloodshed, but also memorable vignettes that paint Jocho in a more anthropomorphic light. While recording Jocho's lectures, I discovered was that he was not much transcribing from the old fella who lives in the rest home down the road. Remembering that the dialogue between Tsuramoto and Jocho took place over seven years, being human, Jocho surely had his good days and bad days. Sometimes he was irate. Sometimes he was jovial. Sometimes he was probably enjoying a few cups of the warm rice wine Tsuramoto brought with him to share on a cold winter's night. In any case, the text displays plenty of humor if you can imagine Jocho grinning away as he pulled one over Tsuramoto. For example, the following lighthearted vignette comes to mind, and I have no qualms about using it to justify a lazy Sunday for myself.

> A man's life is very short, so it is best to do what he enjoys most. It is foolhardy indeed to waste your life in this world between dreams, doing things you don't enjoy as you endure the suffering. I take care when expressing such an opinion. I keep it to myself, lest young samurai hear it and adopt wrong ideas to their detriment. That aside, I like to sleep. Accordingly, I intend to confine myself to my quarters and

spend more time napping.

Maybe it was just a signal for Tsuramoto to go home and leave an old man alone. Maybe it was just his sense of humor. Sometimes we write something as a joke in an e-mail, only to have the recipient take it the wrong way. Interpreting things at face value, or assuming that anything about Bushido must be deadly serious, is a trap that many readers fall into. One of these days, I may just dot *Hagakure* with emoji.

Despite his overbearing cynicism of the new generations of "peace idiots," Jocho was clearly not the total sourpuss he often comes across as. The following conversation must have taken place on a "good day," but it shows that he had a lot of compassion.

> The reason people today lack spirit is that there is peace throughout the realm. They would surely be pluckier as the situation dictates. I don't expect that the men of old were that different from warriors now. Even if they were, that was then. Samurai today are merely in tune with the state of the world, where everything is mediocre compared to before—but that doesn't mean that they are inferior.

Life with No Regrets

The acceptance of death described in *Hagakure* is difficult to imagine for people today, controlled as we are by the impulse to keep questions of mortality far removed from our lives. We are not accustomed to incorporating an awareness of our inevitable mortality into our daily routines. It is nothing if not logical, though, to realize that we are all going to die, and at any moment. We might be struck by a car as we cross the road. We might be inside a building that collapses in an earthquake. Who knows?

I cannot claim to fully understand this. Still, kendo is something that makes me think of death on a daily basis and from many different angles. I do not consider myself morbid. The kendo training that I attend every day makes me contemplate the importance of *sutemi* and making the first cut. I know that not casting away my flesh in a round of mock combat with bamboo swords will lead to being soundly defeated at the hands of a more determined opponent.

Allegorically speaking, *sutemi* in kendo is the same as being "resigned to die." *Sutemi* comes directly from the warrior code of Bushido. *Sutemi* means overcoming the fear of defeat. It is the conviction that, if you are going to go, then go with everything you have. No regrets. It is the understanding that only you can be responsible for your actions. It is the antithesis of half-heartedness.

When I participate in rigorous practice sessions, my field of vision will darken as fatigue sets in. Before long, the threshold of discomfort is crossed, and all my worries and fears dissipate. I feel entirely liberated, in some ways euphoric. Is this what Jocho means by "death frenzy?" I consider training in this way, with this intensity, as a kind of "rehearsal" for death. At least, it makes me think a lot about it. Jocho's outlook suggests that the final moment of our lives is also the apex. By contemplating death, the samurai learned how to live. Is this not an ageless, universal tenet of wisdom?

CHAPTER 4

Live and Let Live: The Life-Giving Sword

Tactics of Restraint

As discussed in Chapter 3, the "bullheaded" and "balmy" Bushido of the Edo period considered mindfulness of death as central to the samurai's ideal course of action, albeit it for different reasons. The *Hagakure* mentality sought single-minded purity in the intent to serve. The Confucian-flavored creed still promoted single-minded resolve to serve, but was more centered on self-development and the preservation of Order.

Another influential school of thought preceded them: the teachings of the shogun's own martial arts instructor, Yagyu Munenori (1571–1646). Along with some of his illustrious contemporaries, such as the scholars of military studies Hojo Ujinaga and Toyama Nobukage, Munenori sought to provide a blueprint for samurai "peace management" by promoting the following idea: the mark of a superior government was a realm devoid of conflict. His classic treatise, called *Heiho-kadensho*, was particularly influential among the elite strata of samurai society, rather than the rank and file. In fact, even Jocho's lord, and his father before him, were students of Munenori's swordsmanship and related philosophy.

Yagyu was teacher to the second and third Tokugawa shoguns, Hidetada and Iemitsu, respectively. He sought advice from the famous Rinzai monk, Takuan Soho, and integrated Zen teachings with Confucianism and concepts of Noh drama into his recipe for warrior deportment in times of conflict and in times of peace. *Heiho-kadensho* is also a catalogue of techniques for the Yagyu Shinkage-ryu tradition of swordsmanship. The deeply esoteric principles underlying his system of combat also served as an aesthetic of governance. *Heiho-kadensho* was originally written for the shogun but became a standard point of reference for many daimyo throughout the country.

Munenori quotes Chinese philosophers such as Laozi and crafts an argument that one can remain a bona fide warrior while also renouncing war. In fact, he maintains that this was the supreme intent of being a warrior. This conceptual reasoning provided light at the end of the tunnel for samurai who were wondering how relevant they were in peacetime. His teachings offered samurai an intellectual foundation for continuing to see themselves as warriors without involvement in armed conflict; in fact, *because* of the absence of conflict.

Teaching professional men of arms to renounce war might appear to be a contradiction in terms. The book contains maxims explaining unconventional tactics such as "fell the enemy without the use of a sword" and "win without fighting." This represents an evolution in martial culture, from the "death-dealing blade" to the "life-giving sword." In this chapter, I examine the minutiae of *Heiho-kadensho* pacifism and spiritualism.

How Not to Be Killed

Heiho-kadensho consists of three chapters: "Shoe-Presenting Bridge," "Death-Dealing Blade," and "Life-Giving Sword." "Shoe-Presenting Bridge" records ideas about the martial arts that were taught in the Shinkage-ryu school of swordsmanship by Munenori's father, Muneyoshi. One of Munenori's chief arguments was that the heart of the swordsman determines victory and defeat, not technical ability. In other words, mental preparation decides the outcome well before the fight begins. He advocates a balance of physical and psychological awareness, and his work is a trailblazing precursor to sports psychology books popular among elite athletes today. In this context, the martial arts were much more than an exercise to nurture skills to fell opponents. The system Munenori taught was concerned primarily with cultivating the mind and spirit through the vehicle of techniques.

The other two chapters initiate the reader into the logic behind juxtaposing principles of swordsmanship and governance. Munenori considers outstanding martial skill to be represented by preparation for unanticipated developments, thereby being ready to mitigate the necessity of military force. Following the traditions of Laozi, he saw the deadly use of force as contravening "the Way of Heaven." "Weapons are unfortunate instruments. The Way of Heaven hates them." Accordingly, the greater a warrior's ability to circumvent violence, the greater his virtue as a leader. Munenori stressed that the avoidance of conflict was not cowardly but, rather, confirmed the highest level of martial ability. Again, I am reminded of the third form in the Nihon Kendo Kata.

He also advises allowing an aggressor attack you if that is his intention.

It is easy to cut a man down with a single blow of a sword. Avoiding a cut, however, is a different matter. If an adversary advances to strike you down, hold control of the interval and, above all, maintain a placid state of mind as you allow him to execute his attack. Even though his intent is to smite you and he goes through the motions to this end, his blade will not reach if you control the distance. His sword will then be rendered ineffective, allowing you to storm over his dead blade and claim victory.

Making the first move in a skirmish is straightforward, but it is difficult to allow the enemy to attack first without getting killed. The underpinning idea is that the warrior should not be the aggressor; but if an antagonist wants your blood on his sword, then you are within your rights (and forgiven by Heaven) to settle the score after he has taken his shot. Doing this, however, requires an incredibly subtle manipulation of the spatial distance between your body and his weapon. It must be close enough for the enemy to feel confident about unleashing his murderous blow, but distant enough to miss by a whisker. Munenori warns the swordsman to keep his wits even after the clash and "under no circumstances stop the mind at the place you have cut." Being distracted would afford your enemy the chance for a second crack of the whip. Ah, yes. *Zanshin.*

No Sword, No Problem

The "Death-Dealing Blade" is the most fundamental level in swordsmanship. Kill or be killed. There is no ambiguity about this.

As explained in the section on Nihon Kendo Kata in Chapter 3, the swordsman must learn to go beyond this basic stage. He first masters a variety of fighting methods as he raises his level of proficiency. If he lives long enough, he will eventually understand the inner-most teachings of swordsmanship. These teachings led many hardened warriors to the realization that conflict was nothing more than bad karma. Munenori's school expressed such attainment in the concepts "Life-Giving Sword" and "No Sword."

"No Sword" is a technique in which, with only your hands as weapons, you still overcome an armed opponent. Your arms will be shorter than the length of a sword, making retreat disadvantageous; but entering the optimal unarmed fighting distance means an imminent danger of being cut down. The secret, said Munenori, was judging the distance to perfection, preempting the attack, and taking hold of the hilt as the sword swooshes past your body in the closest shave known to man. After you take hold of his sword hilt, there is little he can do for the following simple reason:

> If he focuses too much on keeping his sword from being snatched from him, he will forget to strike you. His mind has become so preoccupied with holding on to his sword, that he is unconsciously rendered incapable of attack. If you avoid being cut this way, then you are the victor. Your goal is not to deceive your opponent to remove his sword per se.

That is, you do not have to physically confiscate his blade, but make him attach his mind to it so that it stops there. Confiscation was an option, though:

> "No sword" is not just the art of taking the enemy's sword from him. It can be used to remove all manner of implements at will. If you can take your opponent's sword when you are unarmed, then you can use anything as an effective weapon. For example, you can defeat an opponent armed with a sword with a simple fan. This is the mind-set of "no sword."

Mastery of this concept, in Munenori's estimation, was the highest level achievable in swordsmanship. Letting your arms hang loose, with no sword in hand, and standing nonchalantly before your enemy: At first glance, you might appear to be completely unprepared, but you are never readier for any attack your opponent might bring. From the outset, you are messing with his mind by making him think he has the upper hand. In terms of having a sword, he may have, but the mind is the warrior's greatest weapon. You need absolute control over your own mind to pull off this technique, and it is this psychology of combat espoused by Munenori that is the most interesting. *Heiho-kadensho* was one of the first books in Japan to make the connection with the psychology of individual combat and apply it to other aspects of life and rule.

The creator of the "no sword" teaching was not Munenori but his father, Yagyu Sekishusai Muneyoshi. He was the progenitor of the Yagyu Shinkage-ryu school of swordsmanship later inherited by Munenori. The school was to become one of the most celebrated of the Edo period because of the patronage of successive shoguns and daimyo countrywide. When the Tokugawa Ieyasu first got wind of the Shinkage-ryu's magnificent "no sword" technique, he summoned Muneyoshi to Kyoto to see it for himself.

Ieyasu took his wooden sword against the barehanded Muneyoshi, only to be defeated three times in succession. Far from humiliated, Ieyasu saw in "no sword" intriguing lessons for governance. He pleaded with Muneyoshi to become his official martial arts advisor, but he refused, because he was already sixty-eight years old. Ieyasu pressed him further, so Muneyoshi recommended that his son be given the post instead.

As impressive as it clearly was, if "no sword" were the only idea it contained, *Heiho-kadensho* would be little more than a family record with some arcane lore on swordsmanship. What is most interesting about this book, however, is that this and many other teachings about swordsmanship and military tactics are applicable to far greater situations than a one-on-one duel. This was not lost on Ieyasu and future leaders.

> The ability to understand this and to plot to prevent the personal schemes of a governor, mayor, magistrate, or village head from ruining the land is comparable to the ability to judge your opponent's stratagems by observing his moves in a sword fight. You must be attentive and observant. Something of greater ability can be learned from swordsmanship.

Munenori promoted the idea that a military mind-set was needed for rulers to remain aware of conditions in the realm before it erupts into revolt. "In times of peace, never forget the chaos of war." A prophetic warning against the dastardly "peace stupor" to which later generations would fall victim. Swordsmanship and military tactics were thus vital for keeping the peace. Perhaps one of the most famous exhortations in this respect is in the following passage.

> At times, because of one man's evil, ten thousand people suffer. So, you kill that one man to let the thousands live peacefully. Here, truly, the blade that deals death becomes the sword that gives life.

There is a striking resemblance to "George W. Bushdo" and his justification for ridding the world of the despot Saddam Hussein. Whether this tactic was effective (or even justified) in Iraq given the current state of affairs is, sadly, doubtful. But it was certainly convincing enough for the leaders of the Tokugawa regime. Their existence as warriors in peace was defensible precisely because a sudden vacuum of military power could easily be filled by a psychotic saber rattler who cares less about the "Way of Heaven." Again, perhaps a clichéd justification for any dictatorship or violent revolution, but remember that Japan had just emerged from 150 years of anarchy and for 250 years after this was not involved in any major internal or international conflict. Not bad for a warrior regime. Few countries in the world can claim such an extended era of peace.

Swordsmanship involved two people squaring off. One side wins, anbd the other loses. This is swordsmanship on a micro scale, Munenori tells us, and victory or defeat in such an encounter is not going to sway history. If, however, we are talking about a general and the fate of an entire country, the same principles of swordsmanship and the ability to employ them surely have far-reaching consequences. Remaining abreast of the potential for chaos in society in the same vein as one carefully observes an enemy swordsman, then preempting and cutting mayhem short in its tracks, is the essence of military discipline in peacetime. Therefore, *Heiho-kadensho* is more than just a manual for dueling with swords. It is a packaged political ideology for governance, as well as an advanced discourse into the deepest reaches of the warrior's psychology. Its influence is still very strong in modern kendo for reasons I will outline shortly.

Ainuke and *Kumazasa-no-Oshie*

"No sword" was extolled as a brilliant concept by the most powerful mover and shaker in Japan, Tokugawa Ieyasu. The seemingly ludicrous idea of not using a sword yourself, yet being able to stop your adversary from using his meant that, in the end, no one needs to die. No killing, not being killed, just good old simple living. That is swordsmanship at its highest philosophical level. The Shinkage-ryu school of swordsmanship was founded during the Sengoku period. The zenith of its ideals gleaned through the experiences of war—that is, prevailing through peaceful means—were later adopted by military and Confucian scholars, such as Yamaga Soko and Daidoji Yuzan.

The Edo period had scores of famous swordsmen. One stands out as a truly bizarre, but brilliant specimen—Harigaya Sekiun (?–1669). His student was Odagiri Ichiun (1630–1706). Inspired by his enigmatic guru, Ichiun wrote *Kenpo Sekiun-sensei soden* (Sword Techniques

Taught by Master Sekiun, 1686), a curious book that promotes the concept of *ainuke*—that is, passing through.

> When the swordsmen are of equal caliber and proficiency, the game as it is generally played [in a fencing bout] finishes with an *ai-uchi* [mutual strike], which, when carried on with real steel, means killing each other. An *ainuke,* however, does not at all involve any kind of killing or hurting each other, as *-nuke* means not "striking down" as *uchi* does, but "passing by" or "going through" unhurt.

This enlightened state was premised on the idea of being oblivious to the outcome of the encounter. There is nothing particularly unique about this notion, but Sekiun took it to another plane. He advocated going in for the kill without avoiding the oncoming enemy strike. If it resulted in *aiuchi*, then so be it. Both dead. If the swordsman survives long enough, he will become a sage; sensing this, people will avoid confrontation with him. If another sage happens along, both will know right away that death for both is the imminent outcome, so they pass each other by. This is what is meant by *ainuke*.

This may seem like a wild mental leap, but I associate *ainuke* with the notion of "mutually assured destruction" (MAD) in the nuclear age. In the event of a "first strike," the country under attack can still react in time to achieve nuclear retaliation and hence total obliteration for all concerned. Not exactly a reassuring strategy, counterintuitive in fact, but *ainuke* was the MAD of early-modern Japanese swordsmanship. No doubt, the idea of a win-win situation for both swordsmen through abstention, justified by some unspoken concurrence of futility, was mocked as being genuinely "mad" by those with a more cynical disposition. Jocho immediately comes to mind. It was, it could be argued, just a clever escape route for cowardly pretenders to avoid getting hurt or killed. Skepticism aside, the desire to avoid spilling blood became the supreme teaching of many martial traditions.

For example, another illustrious school of swordsmanship—in fact, the granddaddy of them all—is the Tenshin Shoden Katori Shinto-ryu. It stood by the teaching that "the martial way is the way to peace." If martial arts are meant to be arts of peace, then victory without fighting must be considered the apex. The founder of Tenshin Shoden Katori Shinto-ryu was another genius swordsman called Iizasa Choisai Ienao (1387–1488). He was a true and tested combatant, and his reputation preceded him.

Being famous, however, was troublesome for a martial artist. One never knew when the next challenger would show up, wanting to make a name for himself by toppling the almighty. Tired of a life of dueling dilettantes, he developed a ploy to weed out those unworthy of a genuine lesson in swordsmanship. This is known in the school to this day as the "Kumazasa Bamboo Teaching" (*kumazasa-no-oshie*).

Ienao received his challengers civilly, offering them tea beforehand. He then invited them to see the striped bamboo in the garden, a very thin, malleable variety of bamboo. He would sit atop a bush, but it would not bend under his weight, as if he was levitating. He invited challengers to join him, but to a man they turned on their heels and ran for their lives. Of course, the reader will scoff at such a proposition. We all know that people cannot levitate. Perhaps there was some trick to the performance. Whatever the case, it is of no consequence. The point of the teaching was to defeat challengers without drawing a sword.

In those days, it was not uncommon for adepts of different martial art traditions to duel to the death. Itinerant swordsmen wandered the country on pilgrimages, seeking matches with others to hone their craft. It was a hazardous occupation, but opportunities abounded for swordsmen who stood out. Seeing Ienao's actions, however, aspirants would immediately sense their inadequacy and reconsider their options. It is surely a myth to elevate the status of the founder of the school, but it is a good illustration of Ienao's teaching that the way of war is the way of peace, a doctrine that endures to this day and permeates the modern martial arts.

The true aim of budo, we are still taught, is to nurture people who avoid getting into fights. Instead, they can use their strength and courage for more productive purposes. The strongest martial artist is one capable of winning without fighting. He swallows his pride and eschews violence in the knowledge that the damage he can do is irreversible. He has nothing to prove.

History is replete with martial artists who came to the very same conclusion through a lifetime odyssey of living on a knife's edge. They were good enough to survive and grasp the insight that "winning without fighting" is the definitive philosophy for warriors. That these "sword sages" were proven killers makes their teachings all the more persuasive. The common theme was that they were unafraid of dying; but simultaneously just saw no sense in killing. Reading between the lines again, who would not rather live than die? Who wants to kill?

Who really wants to be killed? Acceptance of something and wanting it are very different things. Samurai were as human as anyone.

Timing the Attack

As fighting with swords is no longer the norm, we generally view concepts such as "no sword" as abstract philosophies with little relevance to contemporary society. It is important to remember, though, that they have their roots in real combat. A master of "no sword" would, unarmed, attack his opponent by knowingly entering the radius of his sword swing. Such a person was prepared for death, should that be his fate. Obviously, it requires considerable mental equanimity to gauge the distance to the millimeter and the timing to perfection. A split second of indecision will end in an eternal siesta.

Heiho-kadensho discusses both martial technique and matters of the heart/mind as two sides of the coin. The body is the vehicle, but the mind is the engine. Mind and body must be in perfect unity for the swordsman to triumph. Your mind, not the adversary, is your worst enemy. Two key terms in explained in *Heiho-kadensho* related to this are: *fudoshin* (immovable heart) or imperturbability, and *heijoshin* (normal state of mind), or presence of mind. To better to understand these psychological states in the martial arts, we must also examine what in kendo is called *mittsu-no-sen* (the three timings for attack).

These timings or initiatives for attack have different names depending on the author, but the concept itself is ubiquitous and incredibly important in modern kendo. Generally speaking, the three are referred to as *sen-sen-no-sen*, *sen-no-sen*, and *go-no-sen*. *Sen-sen-no-sen* is what Miyamoto Musashi called *ken-no-sen*, and what Munenori called *kizen*. If we stick with the translation of *sen* as "initiative," this literally means "initiative [yours] on the initiative [opponent's] to the initiative [yours]." The idea here is to enter within the opponent's range and strike him before he can make his own move. In other words, to preempt your opponent's attack by coaxing him into making it and then smacking it down just as he is about to launch it. You attack more quickly that the opponent's *sen*, thereby forestalling their attack. It is an "active preemptive move."

Sen-no-sen, also known as *senzen-no-sen*, means to know ahead of time what the opponent plans to do and not to let him do it: "initiative [yours] preceding the initiative [opponent's]." When striking, the opponent naturally breaks form. The key here is knowing how to respond to the opponent's moves, the changes in his stance and spirit, and defeat him as he initiates them. It is an "interactive preemptive move."

Other names for *go-no-sen* include *tai-no-sen* and *sengo-no-sen*: "initiative [yours] after the initiative [opponent's]." In other words, allowing the opponent to make his move, enter the sphere of his upswing, and defeat him as he is completing his downswing. Alternatively, you may aim your timing for the instant he completes his move and is unable to transition to the next. This does not mean reacting after the opponent's attack. That would simply be a passive response. It requires a proactive process of luring the opponent in, so that you control the timing. You must convince him that he has no choice but to go for it. If you are simply reflexive and miscue the timing, you will be struck. It is, in essence, a "reactive preemptive move."

The critical problem in a bout is determining when to attack. You may strike when the opponent is not moving. You may strike just as the opponent begins to move. Or you may strike after the opponent has moved. It is difficult for an outsider to distinguish the psychological battle of *sen* between two martial artists. Only the two protagonists really know what is transpiring. When facing a true master, however, you never really know when you are being controlled.

Kendo as Communication

Of the three initiatives, *go-no-sen* is the most sophisticated. Even a person who falls victim to this *sen* has no idea what has just happened. In *Heiho-kadensho*, this timing is referred to as *hyori*, which literally means "front and back," or "double-dealing."

> Double-dealing is the root of strategy. Even when your opponent realizes that your double-dealing is an act of deception, he can't help but fall for it anyway. If your double-dealing successfully takes your opponent in, victory is yours. Even if he isn't falling for your initial deception, follow up with yet another. That way, even an opponent who sees through your double-dealing the first time will succumb to it the second time.

Deliberately expose a weakness to lure the opponent in to attack it. This is what is meant by double-dealing. Munenori explains that such a strategy is used in Buddhism. Calling it *hoben*, the Buddha used "expedient means" of providing provision truths to guide his followers to facilitate an incremental realization of the highest truth. In the Shinto religion, the faith of men is awakened using *shinpi* (mystery). In other words, controlling people's minds (or "guiding" them in the case of religion) without their being aware.

In kendo, a high-ranked expert may assail you by conveying no opening or weakness at all. He will not give an inch and will be like a tank with a gun turret pointed at your face. You believe that an attack would be futile, as there is nothing to strike at, and he is not responsive to any of your probing. The truth is, you are probably being lured into a trap. While you are contemplating this impasse, and your mind is preoccupied with trying to keep confusion at bay, he may move in and strike. But then, he may show an ever-so-subtle chink in his armor, and, before you know it, you are launching a desperate strike to take the prize, only to have it grabbed away from you in pre-, mid-, or post-flight. You took the bait and end up snatching defeat from the jaws of victory. You did not even see it coming.

Your task is to hold your water and work out how to double-deal the double-dealer. That will be the test of how well you have embodied the "three initiatives" and the related factors of timing, distancing, mental preparation, imperturbability, and presence of mind. This is all part of the back and forth with your opponent. It is a form of wordless communication, talking through the tips of the swords. Come what may though, when you do go, it must be with everything you have got—*sutemi*.

Kendo practitioners often travel to train at dojos in other towns and countries. This means fighting in an unfamiliar environment with people you have never met before, as in the pilgrimages by warriors in olden times, but not as dangerous. The objectives are the same, though: to test our mettle out of our comfort zone with people about whom we have no preconceptions. We wear full-face protective masks in kendo, so all we can see of the opponent's face are the eyes between the metal bars. You do not know each other's age, history, grade, or nationality, which is why it is the best way to ascertain one's own true strengths and weaknesses.

As we become stronger and more advanced in kendo, however, it is possible to gauge the level of our opponent as soon as swords are crossed. From the opponent's stance alone, you see clues about his or her style of kendo, attitude, and even personality. This provides information on how to approach this particular kind of opponent, as long as you know how to read it. As you accumulate experience over many years, you learn to identify the double-dealing going on and smell the fear on your opponent's breath, or not, as the case may be. He might be smelling yours. Each bout is like having a deep and meaningful wordless conversation with another human being. In the thick of a kendo match, you might as well be naked because whatever you are hiding will become patently obvious before long.

I have talked mainly about swordsmanship to this point, but the skills involved in reading between the lines and seeing into the soul are equally valid in politics, diplomacy, and business. Even though they had little realistic expectation of seeing real action, Edo-period samurai saw martial arts as a way of training their minds, developing their powers of perception, understanding the mechanics of double-dealing and human psychology, and learning to maintain mental concentration in the face of adversity.

Water of the Heart

Reading an opponent's strengths requires perceptiveness to see the heart of the matter. It also requires the ability not to be read and double-dealt by keeping one's mental and emotional conditions under control. The difficult-to-interpret proverbial "poker face" nurtured by samurai was made possible not by facial paralysis but by fostering a mind of *heijoshin* and *fudoshin*. In his "Five-Ring Scrolls" (*Gorin-no-sho*), for example, Miyamoto Musashi wrote about the importance of *heijoshin*.

> In strategy, the way you hold your mind must not vacillate from what is normal. In both combat and daily life, one must be determined but calm. Deal with any situation without being tense or reckless. Your spirit should be placid and unprejudiced. Even though your spirit is serene, be sure not to let your body ease off. When your body eases off, do not let your spirit abate. The spirit must not be influenced by your body and your body by your spirit. Be not under- or overspirited, as both excess and deficiency in spirit is a sign of weakness. The enemy must not see your spirit.

One must have a mind strong enough to keep emotions in check. If one is not centered, control is all but impossible and will lead to rash actions with an unhappy ending. One of the main considerations in martial arts training is forging internal strength and developing a spiritual bearing that enables us to rise above danger. It might not seem obvious, but this is exactly what Jocho was advocating when he said,

"Live as if you are already dead." This constitutes mental preparation for calamity in the extreme. Any resulting action from this state is, therefore, not as impetuous as it may seem.

There is a saying in kendo: "When fire rages in your chest, use the reservoir of water in your heart to put it out." This aphorism can be interpreted in many ways. "When fire rages in your chest" refers to flames of desire or the kind of burning anxiety you feel when things do not go your way. For example, ambitious people focused on success measured in wealth and position often lose sight of what is truly important. They think only of taking the next step in their career, but it is precisely that blind desire that might destroy them. Their impatience for tangible results will entice them into engaging in impulsive, immoral, or dishonest behavior.

In budo, the process of working toward long-term goals is considered more important than short-term outcomes. In this sense, another objective of training hard every day is to purify the "water of the heart" and keep it from stagnating in order to do this. What, then, is the "water of the heart"? In typical kendo training, we undergo rigorous exercises to perfect our technique and get the mind, body, and sword all working together. Come match time, the immediate task is to employ those skills to the fullest to win. If we focus on winning alone, however, and pump ourselves up with the kind of trash talk typical of a boxing press conference, this equates to fire raging in the chest. We have lost our spiritual equanimity, our centered mind, our *heijoshin*. In the end, the kendo match becomes a pitiful scenario of an unbridled ego seeking worldly validation. If we continue down this road and lose our cool, it will work to the advantage of our opponent.

The opposite of *heijoshin* is relinquishment of control. When the chest grows hot, it exposes a short circuit in the heart's wiring. Leaving it to smolder away is an invitation to trouble, and the voracious desire to win will result in catastrophic failure. For a practitioner of the martial arts, such naked desire is an illness of the mind eliminated only through training. Keeping the "water of the heart" pure—that is, not polluted with avarice and narcissistic cravings—is not just about improving your chances in matches. It is the most important component in living life wholeheartedly. That is why the world of budo has so many keywords that end in *shin*—that is, heart.

Kyo-ku-gi-waku

The Itto-ryu, another illustrious school of swordsmanship patronized by the Tokugawa shoguns, was founded by Ito Ittosai at the end of the Sengoku period. Scrolls containing his teachings describe the loss of *heijoshin* in terms of "seven illnesses of the heart": surprise, fear, confusion, doubt, cowardice, contempt, and arrogance. In *Heiho-kadensho*, the same concept is distilled down to four: surprise, fear, doubt, and hesitation (*kyo-ku-gi-waku*). When the heart is gripped by these mental afflictions in combat, failure is imminent. Both in matches and in practice, these four debilitating mental states—known collectively as the *shikai*—must be expelled completely from the mind to even grip the sword correctly.

A "surprise" is something unexpected in the engagement. When startled, you lose your *heijoshin*, tense up, and freeze like a deer in the headlights. "Fear," for example, may be experienced when facing an opponent who is physically dominating or a phenomenal competitor such as the all-Japan champion. If this causes your spirit to wither, there is no way that you can exhibit your full strength. "Doubt" means being anxious, wondering how your opponent will come at you. This dulls your judgment, raises doubts in your mind about your own ability, and leads to destruction. Lastly, "hesitation" means not knowing how you should respond to an action by the opponent, to the point that your next move falls somehow short. "Is he double-dealing? I bet he is, but if I don't do something he will str…"

All these mental shortcomings arise from overexcitement. No matter whom you are facing or what situation you find yourself in, the inability to knock surprise, fear, doubt, or hesitation on the head will mean that your head is knocked down instead.

Budo training is known for its harsh discipline. The point is to expose the weaknesses of the heart and purge them from your being, or at least mitigate the damage they cause. Of course, this is not something that can be accomplished overnight. After years of training, you start to notice that you are less rattled in matches. By extension, you also become less agitated by the vagaries of daily life as well. The caliber and sustainability of your *heijoshin* is in a completely different league, and is one reason that budo offers more value to the individual than a few trophies on the shelf. This comes from filling your heart with pure water. Stagnant water is expelled as sweat and replenished by gratitude, empathy, and humility. The framework for a lifelong journey of mind-body cultivation is contained in this multidimensional combat-culture compendium.

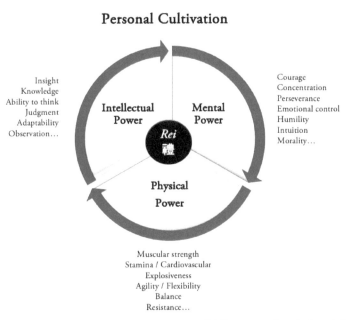

Rei=Respect, empathy and richness in humanity

Many aspects of intellectual, mental, and physical power are gained through the personal cultivation of the mind and body centered around *rei*.

Go with the Flow

If he does not assume the proper "mental stance," even the most gifted swordsman will be surprised by the merest trifle and experience fear, confusion, and doubt. This will cause his heart to "stop." What is meant by this? Seldom does the average person encounter a truly pressing life-or-death situation. Sometimes, however, accidents happen. Mother Nature is always flexing her muscles, and we would be wise to prepare for the worst. Panic, a loss of *heijoshin*, in the face of disaster prevents cogent evaluation in any situation. Samurai were acutely aware of this when they trained their bodies and minds for combat.

Recall *Hagakure*'s notion of the "death frenzy." At the moment of truth, making the appropriate life-or-death decision without hesitation was predicated on a mental state perfectly at ease with adversity. If a samurai's heart "stopped," so, too, would his usefulness. They had to create opportunities to test their grit in adversity. The martial arts became a means of "reenactment," a way to provide a vicarious experience of death to prepare them for any disaster. This is also one of the benefits of studying budo today.

Researchers around the world have long recognized the psychological depth of Japanese budo. The anthropologist Richard Hayes, for example, focused his research on how people react to danger psychologically, self-control, and how all this is affected by training in martial arts. His findings demonstrate that the mental conditions we call *heijoshin* and *fudoshin* are crucial in enhancing combat efficiency.

In scientific terms, the brain emits alpha waves when you are in a relaxed state. Beta waves are connected with a state of alertness but can lead to feelings of anxiety if maintained for too long. Both are important for maximum efficiency, but increasing the alpha-wave state while reducing beta-wave activity is one of the goals of mental training in various fields. The US military, for example, uses neurofeedback to rehabilitate soldiers suffering from post-traumatic stress disorder (PTSD) and brain injuries; and, for performance enhancement, Defense Department researchers are exploring ways of using combat simulators to increase alpha-wave activity in the throes of combat. The brain can be trained to produce brainwave patterns needed for specific needs, and this field is gaining considerable traction. It has been a part of Japanese martial culture for centuries.

In the world of sports, image and mental training involves reaching an alpha-wave state. In psychological terms, this is referred to as the "flow state." For psychologist Mihály Csíkszentmihályi, the concept of "flow" indicates a state of immersion in an activity, also known as "the zone," or "peak experience." Both athletes and martial arts practitioners often experience a state of altered consciousness characterized by heightened concentration, enhanced sensory abilities, perfect self-control, and, sometimes, an altered sense of time.

Having practiced martial arts for many years, I sometimes experienced this flow state. It is as if everything around me is moving in slow motion, and I can see with incredible clarity. You feel as if you cannot lose, and you do not care anyway. This sensation does not come with the flick of a switch, not for me at least, but it is exhilarating when it does. Addictive, in fact.

Unlike most other sports, budo disciplines have their cultural and technical origins in actual man-to-man combat. Budo is not concerned with speed records or hitting balls to the back of a net. It is a clash of wills between two individual protagonists battling each other with mind, body, and technique. It is also a clash of violent proportions, like two beasts locking horns in the wild. There is no half-time, timeouts, or heading to the bench for a rest. The struggle continues until it is decided one way or the other in a "death frenzy" of crashes, clashes and smashes. Both protagonists put everything on the line and enter a sublime state of flow that is emancipating and energizing.

The flow state is still not automatic for me even after three decades of austere kendo training but is becoming so little by little, bout by bout. Kendo is my portal into a discovery of what the mind is capable of. I remember training with a grandmaster of kendo a few years ago. It was the height of summer in Japan, mercilessly hot and humid. He took on each challenger one after the other. When each of them conceded defeat, they would "let go" in one closing death frenzy of relentless attacking. The grandmaster allowed the barrage of strikes to connect as he corrected their form along the way. Each bout would last an average of five minutes. We challengers would end up exhausted and panting uncontrollably after about two or three minutes, but his breathing was even from start to finish. We were excited, and our hearts were suffused by the four illnesses of surprise, fear, doubt, and hesitation. There was no way that we could win against this old master. Even young *kendoka* at their absolute physical prime were ground into the floorboards like wet mops at cleaning time.

Being at the very bottom of the dojo totem pole, I had the job of packing up the master's equipment at the end of training. When I picked up his *kote* (protective gauntlets) to stretch out the leather palms for drying, I found them to be as dry as a bone. For ninety minutes straight, in midsummer, this man had dealt with a constant succession of rabid challengers attacking him with everything they could muster. His gear should have been soaked in sweat. I just could not get my head around it. I realized that he was going with the flow, completely in the zone, and not ruffled in the slightest by our dogged attempts to land a lucky strike. This, I thought, must be *heijoshin*.

Freeing the Spirit

Heiho-kadensho discusses *heijoshin* in the use of weapons and even musical instruments.

> You cannot shoot an arrow accurately if you remain conscious of the act of shooting, nor can you wield a sword effectively if you are conscious of wielding it; brushing calligraphy lucidly cannot be achieved if you are conscious of the act of writing; playing the koto [Japanese harp] precisely is not possible if you are aware of performing. An archer shoots accurately when he is not conscious of shooting and does so with the "everyday mind." You cannot use a sword, ride a horse, write calligraphy, or play the koto without engaging with the everyday mind. … If you become obsessed with one thing, then you have strayed from the Way. … The man of the Way is a mirror; his body-mind and is clear and devoid of attachment. His mind is empty but lacks nothing. It is just an everyday mind. He who can do everything with the "everyday mind" is a true master.

This passage tells us that the secret of success when face to face with the enemy is not to seek success. That is, one should not overthink things and always engage with a calm mind as you would with every mundane task. Of course, this is easier said than done, as it is difficult to fully separate ourselves from our ego and desire for victory. "I'm going to use this technique." "I'm going to watch out for such-and-such a move." This is the ego talking, and this persistent, pervasive mental chatter gives rise to tiny ripples that grow into waves. These waves of attachment cloud judgment and swamp the mind with the "four illnesses of the heart," the antithesis of the "everyday mind."

The passage explains that the closer one gets to becoming a true master in some pursuit, the freer one becomes from the constraints of its established protocols. As Jocho tells us, as the samurai learns to accept death, he is freed of his attachment to life. Freedom from the shackles of one's existence means one can act spontaneously and effectively without a second thought. This is the ultimate "everyday mind" that can be cultivated only by pushing through one's comfort zone to attain a higher realization of the meaning of one's existence.

Ultimately, the old samurai classics tell us, this leads to the paradoxical realization that there is no need to fight. Master swordsmen of the turbulent Sengoku period arrived at this very understanding. In fact, violence was considered highly undesirable. Such men were were regarded not only as formidable warriors tested in battle, but also spiritual leaders who saw the world with clarity and compassion. Lacking attachments, they were "free spirits," and the schools that they created to convey their knowledge were more than systems of combat; they were religions that taught apostles how to live their lives meaningfully on the borrowed time they had in this world. In the Edo period, the martial arts were seen even more as vehicles for self-improvement, and this is very much the cornerstone of modern budo today.

CHAPTER 5

Bushido: The Dark and the Light

Internationalization and Decline

In my estimation, budo is one of Japan's most successful cultural exports. In just about any town in every country in the world, chances are that you will find a dojo there. Karate and judo are clearly the leaders in terms of the number of participants. Kendo, aikido, *jujutsu*, sumo, *kyudo*, *shorinji kempo*, *naginata*, and *kobudo* (classical martial arts) are sprinkled here and there. A plethora of new hybrid martial arts and indigenous fighting systems have also been influenced or stimulated by the popularity of Japanese budo in some way. Hundreds of millions of people around the world are involved in budo in some capacity.

The migration of budo to the West started a little before the turn of the twentieth century. "*Jiujitsu*" (unarmed grappling) was the first Japanese martial art to capture Westerners' imaginations. Even US president Theodore Roosevelt purportedly set up a judo room in the White House. Russian president Vladimir Putin is also an accomplished practitioner of judo, a connection that has certainly not gone unnoticed in Japan. Former French president Jacques Chirac is a known aficionado of sumo. The respect shown to the traditions of budo has done more to promote understanding and amicable grassroots relations with Japan than many could ever imagine. Non-Japanese practitioners are eager to learn about time-honored Japanese etiquette, language, and the "mysterious Japanese spirit" behind it all.

At a typical overseas dojo, one might see the flag of Japan pinned to the wall alongside the national flag of that country. A Japanese sword or kanji scroll may be respectfully displayed at the front, together with photographs of a Japanese master connected to that discipline. The locals will be dressed in a *dogi* (training top), and counting to ten in Japanese as they warm up. They will enact Japanese protocols of politeness as they bow to their *sensei* and each other, over and over. The majority of Japanese people are completely unaware that budo is a textbook example of "soft power." Manga, anime, sushi, *kawaii* (cute), J-Pop, fashion, film, Hello Kitty… they all part of Japan's "gross national cool," but budo is special. Tens of millions more people study budo outside Japan than in it, and because of such a global presence, it should no longer be thought of solely as the cultural domain of Japan.

Budo's situation in Japan, however, is far from rosy. The number of participants is declining across the board. Apart from karate, all other modern budo disciplines are shrinking. Karate is experiencing an upward trend thanks to being selected as an Olympic event for 2020 but was a minority budo in Japan before this. *Kobudo*, the classical martial arts, are becoming an extinct species at an alarming rate. As of 2011, judo had 576,000 registered participants in France, of which about 80 percent were under the age of eighteen, and about 60 percent were under twelve. In Japan, the national judo organization has a meager 170,000 registered members, less than one-third the number in France. Japan's national population is twice that of France, so in per-capita terms, its judo population is almost six times larger.

The country's population is decreasing, so a drop off is in some ways inevitable, but most kids these days would prefer to take up something "cool" such as soccer, baseball, basketball, or volleyball. The number of high school-age participants in any of these sports exceeds all high school budo practitioners combined. Older generations of *budoka* often lament that foreigners display a greater understanding of the manners and customs of budo than young Japanese do. There is a certain degree of lip service here but also a measure of truth.

Even the media are eager to jump on budo "scandals" these days. This was never the case before, but instances of bullying at school clubs, match fixing in sumo, and sexual harassment in judo are now taken up gleefully by media outlets. It takes only one worried parent to leak a smartphone video of a high school kendo teacher showing some "tough love" for all hell to break loose. Budo was always considered sacred territory by the media, but not anymore. This is not necessarily a bad thing, and it is highlighting some alarming trends. The line between strict budo education and excessive violence, however, is a fine one. To the uninitiated, that difference can be impossible to tell, and media-fuelled witch hunts are changing the face of budo. I will try to explain based on my firsthand involvement over the years.

Sacrificial Lamb

I first came to Japan as an exchange student when I was seventeen and enrolled at Inage Municipal High School in Chiba Prefecture. My initiation into kendo was as an extracurricular activity at the school club. I had dabbled in judo in New Zealand as a youngster, but I knew nothing of kendo before coming to Japan. I was surprised to learn that, with a bit of effort, the rank of *shodan* was attainable in a year. We do not wear belts in kendo, but *shodan* is the equivalent of a first degree black belt in judo or karate. What better way to commemorate my year as an exchange student in Japan?

My first impression after joining the club? "Kendo is boring." As an absolute novice, all I was taught was how to strike the air with the bamboo sword. The dojo and equipment reeked of stale sweat. My feet and hands were covered in blisters. My body ached all over because of the unnatural fighting stance holding the bamboo sword in front of the body. After each two-hour session, our teacher would lecture us about the spirit of kendo. We would conclude by chanting in unison "1,000 days of training to forge; 10,000 days to polish; one second for the contest to be decided." I had no idea what any of this meant.

Indeed, every day was a "forge" in which we were hammered into shape. Seven days a week, minimum of two hours a day. On Sundays, we would train from 9:00 am until 6:00 pm. The only days we did not have regular training were for tournaments and training camps! It was tough. Our teacher was a successful competitor through his high school and university years, and, following the traditions in how he was taught, the instruction was merciless. He would thrust the sword into our chests hard enough to knock us down. No matter how quickly we bounced back up in desperation, he would knock us down again, and again. Some students would cry and gasp for breath, but they were too scared to stop. Stopping is never an option in kendo.

His name is Sano Katsura, and I now think of him as one of the greatest teachers I have ever known. In retrospect, he really changed the course of my life, but those unfamiliar with the ways of kendo would be shocked at some of the things we did during training. It really was do or die on many occasions. Of course, no real danger was involved, but you do not know this when you are in the thick of it. Every practice, Sano-*sensei* picked some unfortunate soul to work over (to the relief of the rest of us). My turn as the sacrificial lamb to take one for the team did not arrive until I had been practicing for around six months. I thought he might go easy on me. I was an exchange student after all.

Inage Municipal High School Kendo Club.

No such luck. Today was the day. At the time, I was a mere wisp of a lad. He was a solid, intimidating-looking man, not unlike a Japanese mobster. I charged in for my first attack and managed to knock him back a little—a small victory for me. Riding a wave of ill-founded confidence, I did the same thing and knocked him back another few centimeters. To this point, he liked my positive attitude. Then he returned the favor, and I flew back at least a couple of meters. I had expended all my strength in the first couple of hits and could offer no resistance. He kept pushing me back, and, before I knew it, my back was against the wall. "Give up?" he shrieked. "Like bloody hell!" I whimpered back.

Performing *keiko* during daily practice with a fellow member of the Inage Municipal High School Kendo Club.

Then... he moved in for the kill with an mighty attack to my mask. After a second of confusion, my fight-or-flight instinct kicked in. Woefully, I chose flight and sidestepped his attack. He went straight into the wall, putting a hole in it. It was a cowardly move on my part based on an instinct for self-preservation. I turned away when I should have faced the brunt of it like a man.

He was incensed, and so my hell began. The most horrid training exercise in kendo is called *kakari-geiko* (attack practice), in which the student uses the instructor or senior as a kind of mobile punching bag (one that punches back). The attacker enters "death frenzy" mode and goes nuts, attacking all the target areas in rapid succession while shouting at the top of his lungs. Each round usually lasts for twenty seconds, a couple of minutes at most. But not always… Imagine sprinting 100 meters while shouting the whole way. Now imagine doing that with 10 kg. of kendo equipment, a stifling mask covering your face, and thinking that you are going to sprint 100 meters, but it turns out to be 10,000. Let us add a few hurdles to trip you up. And let us not forget the humidity and heat of the Japanese summer.

That's *kakari-geiko*. It is an exercise designed to build strength in body and mind and fluidity in technique. It is the staple diet of *kendoka*. You go until you are given the okay by the senior to stop or until you drop—in which case, you get back up again and keep going. Otherwise, who knows where that bamboo sword will end up! It is absolutely exhausting, but that is the point.

Knocked down, yelled at, struggling to get back on my feet. Hit again. Jumped on. Forced back up to keep attacking, then knocked down again… No mercy, no end. I hated myself for ducking at the last second. Why didn't I just stand my ground? Too late to repent. Penance comes with blood, sweat, and tears. And there was plenty. Yes, even blood, oozing out of my ripped bare feet, and my urine later was a dark color.

From that moment, I "died" in the figurative sense, several times over. I just did not care what happened to me anymore and started drifting away. The only thing on my mind was getting one more strike, and one more, and one more. Every strike was made with all I had to give. Pure *sutemi*. I dropped to the ground, but from somewhere, I would gain a surge of new energy, and the frenzy would start again. Over and over.

Sano-*sensei* eventually stopped me with an uncharacteristically kind comment. "Yup. Good work." The dojo clock read 17:45. I had started at 17:00. It was the first time I had ever experienced anything like it. If it had been New Zealand, then somebody would surely have been arrested. Somehow, though, extreme fatigue and dehydration aside, I felt on top of the world. I felt high on life, liberated, as if I had floated into another universe, riding some mysterious kind of religious experience. I had never been pushed beyond my self-imposed limits to such an extent before, and it was probably my first real foray into the "zone." From that moment on, kendo became an important part of my life. I was well and truly hooked.

Starting Afresh

Ever since then, I have taken practice seriously and have never once wanted to skip out. Summers in Japan are still hell, and dehydration can be a serious problem. The tougher the practice, however, the more it fills me with indescribable satisfaction. I get a feeling of confidence and achievement. "Today, I won—against myself."

Before returning to New Zealand, I shaved my head like the rest of my clubmates and took the *shodan* test. I returned to my home country with *shodan* certificate in hand and a set of armor gifted by my school. Admittedly, I was relieved to have time off, but going cold turkey snapped me out of that pretty quickly. I missed the tension and excitement. The feeling of dread before training and the elation that came with the final call to finish. I missed the sound of bamboo swords clashing. I even missed the stench of stale sweat.

A smattering of kendo could be found in some areas of New Zealand but not in my hometown of Christchurch. A spotty eighteen-year-old who had reached the dizzying heights of *shodan* could do only one thing: I decided to start my own dojo and was put in touch with two people interested in kendo. The year was 1988.

The other two were beginners. I was the only one who really knew anything, so it was up to me to teach at the "Sei Tou Ken Yu Kai," so named by Sano-*sensei* using the same kanji as the high school I attended. I made some pamphlets professing kendo's benefits along the lines of "building endurance" and "good manners." Marketing was obviously not my forte, but before long we had six students. I contacted the Auckland-based New Zealand Kendo Federation, and our little group became affiliated with the family of Kiwi kendo enthusiasts.

Older members, who were in their twenties and thirties and already had budo experience, asked me about Bushido and how it related to the kendo mind. I had no answers. I had never thought about it before. Many of the people who came to watch our practice sessions equated kendo with the "spirit of the samurai" and were looking for something more spiritual, something genuine to samurai culture that

The "Sei Tou Ken Yu Kai" in New Zealand.

they could not find in other martial arts. I was certainly not qualified to pontificate on such matters, but it sparked a sense of urgency in me. I needed to learn more about this "Bushido thing" so that I could at least hold my own in conversation.

As laughable as it seems now, I started by reading the English translation of Yoshikawa Eiji's classic novel *Musashi*. After practice, I quoted phrases from the book but had no real idea what they meant. It was way beyond me. The book gave me a distorted, romantic view of the life of a samurai, but it did pique my interest in warrior philosophy and its many paradoxes. What does it mean to be a warrior? What does it mean to value honor more than your own life? And what on earth does all this have to do with kendo? Before long, I decided to return to Japan to get to the bottom of it all.

Bunbu Ryodo

Most of the rituals in budo, such as bowing, are customary facets of Japanese culture. For Japanese, the ways to act in a dojo—deferential modes of speaking to elders, age-based hierarchy, bowing like bobble-headed figurines to people and inanimate objects—are never questioned because they are all commonplace. Even if a Japanese practitioner does not know the reason for some attitude or action, it is simply accepted. It is what it is, and always has been. For a non-Japanese, however, budo protocols are far from "commonplace." I had no cultural basis for comprehending a lot of what went on. Having taught kendo for a short time in New Zealand and being bombarded with troublesome questions, all I really knew with confidence was how much I did not know.

When I returned to Japan, I studied for six months at the newly established International Budo University (IBU) in Katsuura, Chiba. All I did was practice kendo. The university kendo club boasted over 500 members, all of whom trained at the same time every day in two massive dojos. I also took classes on the history and philosophy of budo, and my professors were more than happy to give me remedial lessons. Those were happy days.

My passion for learning budo burned hotter after finishing the program at IBU. I wanted to stay in Japan and keep digging away but was faced with annoying visa issues. Out of the blue, I was invited to work as the international liaison officer for the All Japan Naginata Federation (AJNF) in preparation for launching the International Naginata Federation in 1990. The AJNF was located in Itami, near Osaka. It was the perfect job for me. I got visa sponsorship and was given free room and board in a dormitory attached to the Shubukan Dojo. The Shubukan is over 300 years old, and I could study kendo, *iaido*, *naginata*, and *kobudo* every day of the week under the tutelage of renowned masters for each discipline. The AJNF office was right next door.

Most of my duties revolved around translation work. Rendering budo concepts into English required a solid understanding of Japanese language, history, and culture, not to mention budo. I bumbled my way through the work for a year and found my calling through the experience. After returning to New Zealand in 1991, I studied Japanese and East Asian history at the University of Canterbury and embarked on a career in academia.

Several times a week, I trained at the kendo club that I founded a few years earlier, slightly better equipped to pass on the knowledge I had learned in Japan. I did not want to teach though. I wanted to learn and knew that I had to head back to Japan. I managed to procure a Japanese government scholarship in 1995 to conduct graduate work in the Department of Japanese History at Kyoto University. My master's thesis focused on the samurai ethos described in the *Koyo-gunkan*.

The next step was a doctorate, but it was not easy finding a suitable advisor. Orthodox historians do not consider "Bushido" a serious field of inquiry. The academics I approached in Kyoto University's history department seemed to have a strong aversion to the idea. To them, the topic was pseudo-research colored with hints of ultranationalist militarism. You only need to look at me to know I am not a Japanese ultranationalist, which made my research plan seem even more pie-in-the-sky. Use of the word "Bushido" is accepted across the board in Japan in the context of popular culture but not as a serious field of scholastic investigation, especially at a traditionally slightly left-of-center institution of higher learning such as Kyoto University. Historians refused to entertain my ideas, but fortunately a professor of Japanese theology was interested in overseeing my research, mainly because he was an advocate of fieldwork and believed that a non-Japanese who actually did kendo could offer some unique perspectives hitherto overlooked.

Transcending Victory and Defeat

I read hundreds of books dealing with Confucianism, Buddhism, Shinto, military history, and strategy. I slogged my way through primary sources, beginning with *Koyo-gunkan*, samurai diaries, historical epics such as *Taiheiki*, and essays by samurai scholars, such as Yamaga Soko and Hayashi Razan. I wrote a PhD dissertation in Japanese, which was later published as *Bushi no etosu to sono ayumi* (The Bushi Ethos and Its Evolution: An Examination of Bushido through the History of Social Thought; Shibunkaku, 2008).

As my supervisor predicted, my practice of budo helped a great deal in understanding the samurai mind. To gain this understanding required the physical, technical, and emotional experience of budo. Some aspects of the samurai mind, predicated as much as it was in personal combat, can be sensed only with flesh and blood.

Although my initial objective for studying samurai thought was to make sense of the concealed implications and potential of budo as a journey toward self-perfection, I discovered that the opposite was also true. Budo helped me see aspects of the samurai mind that would otherwise have remained hidden from view. Of course, the styles of swordsmanship practiced then and now are very different, as are the lifestyle and values; but the core knowledge, the DNA of Bushido, has been preserved in the resin of *keiko*. *Keiko* is a designation for "training" in martial arts. It literally means "to consider ancient knowledge," to shed light on the present.

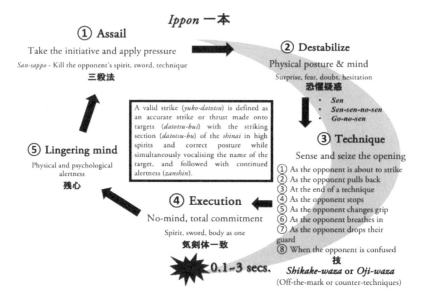

The process of executing *ippon* with *zanshin* in five steps.

Modern *kendoka* are taught that bamboo practice swords must be afforded the same level of respect as real blades. Kendo matches involve considerably more failed strikes than successful ones. How can this come close to resembling combat with real swords? In terms of the reality that a blow from a *shinai* (bamboo sword) is never going to be fatal in the literal sense, it cannot. But the *kendoka* strives to make that one decisive cut with a unity of sword, body, and mind. The first cut is the deepest, whether yours or your opponent's, and the perfect *ippon*—executed as if one's life depends on it—is lauded as the highest aesthetic and the philosophical bedrock of modern kendo.

According to the late Nakabayashi Shinji, a giant of budo studies, the question of victory and defeat premised on life and death is at the very crux of budo. Thus victory or defeat in the sporting sense of modern budo is still philosophically associated with death. In a modern kendo match, a near-miss or glancing blow does not constitute a point but theoretically would still result in death. This notion derives from the traditional budo thinking that its true value is in becoming equipped not merely with the skills to win, but also with the mind to overcome questions of life and death.

Budo is undoubtedly aggressive. The intention now is to win, but in the past it was to stay alive. Each competitor attempts to overcome the opponent and deny him the opportunity for success. The budo practitioner must learn not to be afraid of the opponent, and at the same time, must not despise nor look down on him. With this understanding, the protagonists embroiled in a violent exchange of techniques have a common interest. Each is obligated to fight with all his or her might, without holding back and without hiding anything. It may seem "animalistic," but through these extreme encounters the practitioner learns that the reasons for success or failure lie in the self. The opponent is a medium for confronting one's own weaknesses and deficiencies, through cooperating for mutual advancement. The more intense the exchange, as I found out, the deeper the bond that forms, and the more appreciative one becomes. That is the paradox, and ultimately the beauty of budo.

Thus, many aspects of budo have little to do with competition per se. Budo is a very broad culture with value for everyone at every stage of life, from youth to old age. In the end, budo is a path for learning how to be yourself. If someone were to ask me now, "What is the true nature of budo?" I would answer along the lines, "Based on the philosophical tenets of Bushido, budo is an interminable spiritual journey of self-discovery—a path traversed by throwing yourself body and soul into practice with a mind that transcends questions of life and death."

Materials for the Spiritual Pursuit

I train with what I call the "three Ks" in mind: *keiko* (training), *kenkyo* (humility), and *kufu* (correction). It goes without saying that, in *keiko*, not just masters but even the most inexperienced in the dojo can teach you many things. Humility to accept any lessons from the most unlikely source is an essential element. You will often find those with a smidgen of advanced knowledge champing at the bit to show it off. They are always keen to teach but less inclined to be taught, unless it is by the head of the dojo. Being confident of your ability also requires being conscious of your shortcomings. Letting advice percolate in your mind to see whether it might help you overcome another hurdle is what is meant by "correction."

Your personality traits and current state of mind become apparent during training. You may be bold one day but uncertain the next.

You might be punishing the following day but puny the next. Every day is different, and the more you learn about budo, the more you learn about yourself. It is not always nice, but the objective is a quest for perfection. Over the years, my attitude toward everyday living, including my interaction with others, has been profoundly influenced by budo. It has become the central guiding principle for my view of the world. Kendo is not a hobby or pastime; it is my religion.

I personally know hundreds of *kendoka* around the world. It has always saddened me that foreign practitioners lack the resources and information needed to guide them on their way up the mountain path. The historical processes that influenced budo's evolution over many centuries are particularly misunderstood. Budo is absolutely an extension of samurai culture, but what we do in the dojo now is not the same as what the samurai did, despite the terminology and rhetoric that suggest it is. Many people want to believe that it is. It is not.

If people knew more about the way in which budo culture has been constantly adjusted to remain relevant through the ages, they would be able to embrace more realistic ideas about what can be gained from it, and reconcile many of the apparent contradictions that permeate martial arts in the modern era. Through writing my second PhD dissertation, completed at the University of Canterbury in 2012, I came to know a great deal more about the history of swordsmanship and its educational value. I wrote the dissertation for my own edification, with the intention of sharing my findings with non-Japanese-speaking budo aficionados who cannot access the treasure trove of primary sources and other documents. This thesis was published as *Kendo: Culture of the Sword* by the University of California Press in 2015.

Fifteen years earlier, I was involved in another enterprise to fill the knowledge vacuum. The Japan-based International Kendo Federation (FIK) was established in 1970. Kendo information emanating from Japan is limited in volume and quality. Several booklets for technical instruction—many of which I was called upon to translate—are available, but there are few materials in any other language other than Japanese that provide a detailed account of kendo's background, culture, history, spirit, and philosophy. Of the books that do exist on kendo and budo culture, mistranslation is a constant problem. I have been lucky enough to have lived and studied in Japan for over half my life. I am blessed with regular opportunities to meet and train with Japan's top experts. This is what prompted me to start an English-language magazine devoted to kendo.

Kendo World is published twice a year with the subtitle "Crossing Swords & Borders." The first issue was put out at the end of 2001, at eighty pages. It had articles about the history of kendo equipment tracing back to the eighteenth century, the connection between Buddhism and meditating in kendo before and after practice, and various other obscure topics. We received positive feedback, and our international circulation grew by leaps and bounds. We also publish books and DVDs to make specialized information available outside Japan. What little profit we make we use to promote kendo further.

Why Take Up Budo?

I worked as an assistant professor at the International Research Center for Japanese Studies, in Kyoto from 2002. Nichibunken, as it is known, is a veritable theme park for academic endeavor. After my four-year contract expired, I taught comparative culture, Japanese history, and budo at Teikyo University. Now I teach the same topics at Kansai University in Osaka. One consistent area of research over the course of my career has been the internationalization of budo. I explore why are more and more non-Japanese are taking an interest in Japanese martial arts. I have traveled the world visiting dojos and budo groups in many countries, training, drinking, and waxing lyrical about the martial ways. I have collated extensive data from enthusiasts and believe that non-Japanese take up budo based on twelve main motivations. Of course, there is considerable overlap, and motivations do change over time.

1. As a competitive sport (Olympics participation, etc.)

2. To learn fighting skills and self-defense (police, military, bullying, personal empowerment, etc.)

3. Health maintenance (physical and mental well-being, general fitness, etc.)

4. Interest in Japanese culture (anime, pop culture, traditional culture, etc.)

5. Nikkei communities in Pan-America (connection with Japanese heritage)

6. Former Japanese colonies (South Korea and Taiwan)

7. Business and management strategy (especially during the bubble era of Japan's economy)

8. Interest in Eastern ideals and spiritualism

9. Interest in weapons (sword collectors, etc.)

10. Social prestige (prowess through strength, desire to be a master, being involved in running a group connected with Japan)

11. Socializing (desire to belong to a group)

12. Commercial motivations (running kendo dojo to make a living is an increasing trend in China and some European countries, for example)

Vitamin R

Of the reasons on this list, number 8 is of particular interest to me. Although motivations for starting budo vary, depending on age and environment, many people I have talked to report that the embryonic spiritual or religious countenance of the martial arts has taken on more significance for them over time.

In 2004, I spent a few months in Iran to conduct research on Iranian consciousness of Japanese culture, with a focus on the martial arts. I was taken aback by how enthusiastic Iranians are about the martial arts. According to the editor of one of six specialist magazines there, martial arts collectively are second only to soccer in terms of the number of participants. The physical education department at Iran's Ministry of Education even established a separate section to administer martial arts. There are dojos everywhere, and Tehran boasts its own giant martial arts complex that even Japan would be proud of.

One night, I was taken to an aikido dojo where they had made their own tatami mats. On the wall in the dojo hung a photograph of the Ayatollah Ruhollah Khomeini, along with portraits of hallowed Japanese budo pioneers, such as Funakoshi Gichin (karate), Ueshiba Morihei (aikido), Kano Jigoro (judo). To my utter surprise, I found out that the dojo I had just visited was inside the former US embassy. During the Iranian Revolution of 1979, students from Tehran University held US embassy staff hostage for 444 days. That very building now houses a museum with displays exposing the wicked ways of the West, a military office (hence the machine gun-toting guards loitering ominously outside), and a dojo for teaching Japanese martial arts.

I found the Iranian people deeply devout in their Islamic beliefs, but not overly fond of the clerics who run the country on their behalf. I was curious to know whether the martial arts, with the many teachings on morality and character development, present any conflict with their Muslim beliefs. I surveyed about 500 people, and the overwhelming majority believed that budo was complimentary to their religion. Comments such as "Budo makes me a better Muslim because the combination of physical and mental discipline helps me to become a better person" were common. One observation that sticks in my mind is representative of the overall sentiment: "Martial arts are like a supplement for me; like vitamins for my faith."

If martial arts can be viewed as "vitamins for faith" in such a devout Muslim country, what about other countries? Budo is increasingly being seen as a sort of "substitute" for religion. I am not necessarily saying that budo is a religion, although that depends entirely on one's definition. In recent years, however, as the appeal of Zen and other East Asian religions and philosophy has increased around the world, I wonder whether budo, as practiced by some people, could be included in the holistic genre of "new religion."

A significant number of people are turning to martial arts to explore their inner selves and to discover a spiritual stanchion to support their lives. I include myself in this group. Evidence of this can be seen in the high-volume of (often questionable) English translations of books on budo and their long-lasting presence in the marketplace. Nitobe Inazo's *Bushido: The Soul of Japan*, Miyamoto Musashi's *Gorin-no-sho* (Book of Five Rings), Daidoji Yuzan's *Budo-shoshinshu* (The Code of the Warrior), Yagyu Munenori's *Heiho-kadensho*, and Yamamoto Jocho's *Hagakure* are representative examples, but are merely a drop in the bucket. Such impetuses are still marginal, but with the increase of secularism around the world, fertile grounds are being formed for alternative modes of spirituality and religion.

The world's 1.1 billion atheists may have no interest in becoming ensconced in the hierarchy of orthodox or new-age religiosity, but most human beings want some kind of spiritual fulcrum. Many are dissatisfied with both new and old religions, and budo may present a new option for those with no religious affiliation. Called "nones," they are growing in number. "Nones" are now the second-largest "religious" group in most of Europe and North America. Budo offers a framework for one's own personal philosophy as a perpetual spiritual journey of self-discovery, and seems to have found a niche in both fundamentalist and secularist societies alike. It just seems to fit in.

Budo Mysticism

East Asian culture is often portrayed as exotic and unknowable. Contributing to this image is a well-known book called *Zen in the Art of Archery*, published in 1948 by the German philosopher Eugen Herrigel. While living and teaching in Japan from 1924 to 1929, Herrigel writes of his journey to achieve a state of "no mind" through the study of archery. He tried to rid himself of attachment and developed a belief in the supremacy of logic. The book popularized the somewhat spurious notion of an inextricable connection between Zen and archery. Herrigel was influenced by his enigmatic teacher, Awa Kenzo, who was viewed as something of a maverick in the world of *kyudo* through his promotion of spiritualism through archery. Even if *kyudo* was not directly affiliated with Zen per se, the quest for psychological equanimity in the shoot, however, does have much in common with Zen ideals.

Even the exceedingly rational Kano Jigoro did not entirely mitigate images of spirituality in his judo as it became known outside Japan. The ability to fight someone much larger and throw him effortlessly through the air was an awesome sight to behold for foreign audiences enjoying his demonstrations. It spoke of a deep spirituality that seemed to transcend mere technical skill.

Without question, spirituality sits at the heart of modern budo, as indeed it did in the *kobudo* traditions of the feudal era. In all of the budo disciplines, the principal goal of the practitioner is to find liberation from random, intrusive thoughts. That is the state of "no mind" that allows the arrow, sword, or fist to fly true to the target.

Of course, Western sports have a spiritual side, too. Pierre de Coubertin, founder of the modern Olympic movement, said, "The duty and the essence of the athlete is to know himself, to control himself, and to outdo himself." He emphasized fair play and the importance of participation over winning at all costs. Although "spiritual" is not a term usually associated with sports, such aspects are definitely present.

Recall Chapter 4, where I introduced the research of Mihály Csíkszentmihályi. He calls active absorption in a physical activity, where consciousness of the self and surrounds dissipates, "flow." Elite athletes speak of their experiences in being locked into "flow" and achieving a state of inner peace in which they step beyond their usual psychosomatic entropy and somehow silence the white noise that fills their minds.

Spirituality is a term that is often bandied about in budo, however, and much of the jargon points toward seemingly irrational otherworldly zones. Use of the Buddhist term *shugyo* to denote the practice of martial arts attests to its cosmic characteristics. Budo is not a religion in the conventional sense but, at its root as a medium for self-perfection, is an explicit view of the relationship between mind and body. They are not ontologically distinct, and the quest for mind-technique-body (*shin-gi-tai*) unification is like enlightenment in Buddhism more than an essential relation. In this way, psychophysical perception cannot be honed through intellectual theorizing, but through forging the

Pre-training meditation (*mokuso*) to focus and clear the mind at the *Kendo World* training camp.

body to free the mind. This in turn affects every aspect of one's outlook on life. Knowledge of such philosophies spread to the West in the postwar era, and it has become common for athletes, who traditionally viewed the body and mind as separate entities, to integrate Zen-like meditation into their training.

Cultural Connector

Competition is most certainly a fundamental reason for budo's popularity abroad, but it is the promise of spiritual fulfillment, something immutable, that sparks people's imagination. In Japan, there is a tendency to view budo as important because it is "traditional culture." Indeed, the cultural milieu of Japan was the crucible in which budo evolved, but I do not study it because it is traditionally Japanese. The attraction for me is in its universal value—some latent human power that functions the same everywhere. Its true value, its essence, transcends countries and geographic regions, religion, and culture.

In addition to taking root overseas, budo has also catalyzed a resurgence in indigenous martial arts around the world. It provides a blueprint for expressing spirituality through various concepts, and even has a tangible method for gauging progress with the belt-rank system. Such things are useful and easily incorporated into non-Japanese martial arts as well.

Japanese budo has also burgeoned abroad in forms that do not exist in Japan. For example, with the recent popularity of mixed martial arts (MMA) and Ultimate Fighting Championship (UFC), even people uninterested in martial arts have probably heard of Brazilian or Gracie jiujitsu. Also, following the widespread popularity of *jujutsu* in the West in the early twentieth century, a hybrid sporting version became established, especially in Europe, which functions as a dynamic sport with sparring and kata, and as a means for self-defense. Germany alone has over 90,000 adherents, and it is a contested event at the World Games. It has much in common with Japanese *jujutsu*, including white uniforms and colored belts, but it is virtually unknown in Japan. A smattering of practitioners exist in Japan, but they are mainly of Brazilian descent.

Thus, budo has grown into something much bigger than the rubric of traditional Japanese culture. A salient feature of budo is its universal appeal, and its predilection for assimilating to different cultures and having meaning for people of all ages and creeds. Budo successfully links cultures and people in ways that few people in Japan have the slightest inkling about. To make a sweeping statement, many budo aficionados in Japan are more concerned about cultural proprietorship and maintaining a semblance of Japanese "purity," rather than acknowledging the bigger, more exciting reality of budo's international migration.

We human beings have more in common than we like to admit when it comes to asserting ethnic and cultural distinctiveness. The core principle of an honorable death in Bushido, for example, is by no means unique to Japan. Death in battle is respected and eulogized as the "ultimate sacrifice" and is on display everywhere. While visiting Italy some years back for the World Kendo Championships, I was intrigued by the countless bronze sculptures of mounted knights and nobles. Tourist guides tell you of a hidden code in the horse's pose that indicates how the rider died. If the horse is rearing on its hind legs, the horseman was killed in action. If one front leg is raised, it signifies that he later died of his wounds. If all four legs are on the ground, he apparently died of natural causes. I have been unable to corroborate this, but—romantic myth or not—it still indicates a penchant for celebrating heroic moments of death as a testament to an individual's contribution to whatever cause.

The virtues of loyalty and filial piety are ubiquitous in the human experience, not just in countries that adhere to the traditions of Confucianism. Sticking with Italy, the mafia certainly comes to mind as a subculture in which loyalty is the highest priority in the most *Hagakure* of ways. And heaven help someone who defames a mafioso's mother! In any case, my point here is directed more at Japanese readers, as there is an exasperating tendency to highlight the uniqueness of Japanese culture, rather than its shared commonality with other human experience. Budo, in my opinion, is living proof of this.

Victory Above All?

I have given a general overview of how and why budo has taken root outside Japan. However, in Japan, budo is facing a crisis. I sensed this when I saw superficial differences in the budo overseas compared to what I knew and practiced in Japan. I initially thought that budo in the West had diverged from the correct path. Then it occurred to me that perhaps it was budo in Japan that was losing its way, albeit camouflaged by the constant barrage of hypocritical rhetoric bewailing the opposite.

The proclivity of the "powers that be" in Japan, for example, to prize victory above all else is a case in point. The official position is that it is not about winning and losing. The reality is that match performance makes all the difference in the budo athlete's future prospects. Results in the arena decide the high school, college, and ultimately company or career a *budoka* may be offered. For this reason, strategies on "how to win" outweigh considerations of character development.

In previous chapters, I pointed out the natural progression for learning budo in which practitioners must first learn how to win. They gradually figure out how to apply the values of budo to their personal philosophy and actions through accumulating life experience. What bothers me about the status quo in Japan now is the growing apathy toward the core values of budo: respect for the opponent, humility, and proper manners.

Judo, for example, has an enduring fixation with how many gold medals can be claimed at the Olympics and other international competitions. At the Beijing Olympics in 2008, the Japanese competitor Ishii Satoshi won the men's gold medal in the 100+ kg. category. He immediately retired from amateur judo at the tender age of twenty-two to become a professional MMA fighter. As the golden boy of judo, he was criticized severely and publicly by the Japanese federation for his decision to go professional. A coveted Olympic gold medal is the highest aspiration and expectation in judo in Japan. He had achieved that. Building character was never a priority for him or his teachers. Getting the desired results was all that counted, and, after he won his gold medal, nothing was left for him to do as an amateur athlete. How can he be blamed for moving on? Good luck to him.

Recently, the chairman of the Federation of Collegiate Kendo lamented to me that character development has been given short shrift at university clubs in recent years. As proof of this, the organization struggles each year to find venues for student tournaments because of their terrible reputation among sports facility administrators. University kendoists fail to clean up after themselves, and generally have little respect for the venue. Judo is not much better from all accounts.

The true test of a *budoka* is how he conducts himself outside the dojo. People pay lip service to the need for good manners and respect, but young practitioners who put that into practice are regrettably becoming few and far between. Ironically, at least from the Japanese perspective, it may be that non-Japanese *budoka* are more mindful of manners, are better at interacting respectfully with others, and are more interested in character development through budo than their Japanese counterparts.

Even so, Japanese tend to criticize budo outside Japan as being obsessed with competition, and is therefore a "debased version of the genuine article." Alas, I have witnessed countless non-Japanese *budoka* who come to Japan for their budo odyssey, only to return home disillusioned and disappointed by the duplicity.

Why Bow?

How can foreign *budoka* demonstrate a greater appreciation for traditional ideals than Japanese practitioners? For non-Japanese *budoka*, even the simple act of bowing as a greeting is not the norm in their own countries. For Japanese people, however, bowing is done hundreds of times a day without a second thought. Those not raised with this custom need an explanation of the significance of bowing. Why must I bow politely to opponents before a match? Why must I bow again after the match? Why must I bow to the *shomen* altar at the beginning and end of training? Why must I go barefoot in the dojo? Why must I follow directives from my seniors who are weaker than me? The list of questions is endless, but they would not even cross the mind of a Japanese person in the dojo. Through this process, perhaps counter intuitively, the non-Japanese practitioner ends up with a stronger commitment to matters of etiquette, almost to the point of excess. At least, this has been my experience.

Methods for teaching judo are very advanced in France and Germany. Approaches for instructing children are painstakingly developed and reviewed to suit the temperament of youth there. In Japan, budo pedagogy is based on "tradition," and even the most outdated ideas are justified simply because "that's the way we've always done it." *Budoka* outside Japan used to follow the Japanese example, but learned to adapt or vindicate the various conventions to fit their own social setting for the sake of relevance and effective dissemination.

Bowing to the *shomen* altar at the front of the dojo.

In France, for example, judo is publicized as a sport with "high educational value." Some campaigns use cartoon characters to illustrate eight virtues one might master through judo: *la politesse* (good manners), *le courage* (courage), *la sincerité* (sincerity), *l'honneur* (honor), *la modestie* (humility), *le respect* (respect), *le contrôle de soi* (self-control), and *l'amitié* (friendship). In other words, parents and children are told that they can experience the joy of self-expression through judo with a moderate degree of self-regulation, all while having fun. I know through personal contact with Yamashita Yasuhiro that Japanese judo authorities are looking to France and other countries for ideas on how they can reinvigorate the educational potential of judo in Japan, as per Kano Jigoro's original ideals. Two decades ago, this would have been considered preposterous.

Another telltale factor demonstrating budo's decline in Japan is the number of people who take it up of their own accord. Outside Japan, adults or children often start budo of their own volition. Parents may make recommendations but ultimately respect the child's right to make up their own mind. In Japan, however, practicing parents have a tendency to coerce a reluctant child into doing budo and follow in their own footsteps. The parents, in turn, are of a generation forced to take it up by their parents in the hope that they would learn discipline, determination, and manners. This may have worked in previous generations, but kids in Japan are generally less compliant now and go through the motions only because they have to. They do not understand why they should be involved and lack a sense of purpose, especially if the teacher bombards them with sanctimonious lectures about "being a better human being" through budo. Thus, teachers are becoming disinclined to push this side of things. Instead, the easiest way to keep everybody happy is by finding ways to succeed in tournaments.

Most kids in Japan see budo as laborious, straitlaced, and hard beyond the call of duty. For the same amount of effort, they would rather play soccer or baseball. At least in these sports they have a chance of becoming superstars someday. Budo cannot match this. Budo is failing to capture the imagination of parents or children nowadays, so the practicing population is shrinking. The administrators of budo in Japan have been unsuccessful in keeping abreast of the changing times, changing lifestyles, and changes in the tastes and temperament of youth.

Budo and Corporal Punishment

One event that exemplifies how the times have left budo behind took place in January 2013: the corporal punishment scandal in women's judo. Reports reached the Japan Olympic Committee about acts of abuse committed by the manager against fifteen elite members of the Japanese women's judo squad. At a training camp to prepare for the Olympics, the women were slapped and struck with bamboo swords and verbally abused.

The media seized on the incident and confirmed that top-level judo instructors were still using draconian methods. The squad members themselves complained to the federation several times, which is evidence of changing social values. Students complaining about their coaches was unheard of until this news broke. In many ways, the budo world is a curiosity, a closed society that admits little fresh air and uses "tradition" as an excuse for its lack of innovation. This incident, however, is one of several in recent years that is exposing budo's dirty laundry.

The women's judo affair prompted a vigorous discussion on outdated instruction methods and corporal punishment, and the mind-set of abuse. The manager in question was a product of his own learning path. He is not necessarily a bad man, but he certainly failed to read the signs as an instructor. I should add that this kind of incident is not limited to budo. All sports in Japan have traditionally been enmeshed in a "cruel to be kind," "no pain, no gain" teaching mentality that can easily get out of hand.

Having been through the system in Japan myself, I must confess that I am not opposed to hard training if it is meted out judiciously. Therein lies the problem. Instruction needs to be "hard" in order to teach practitioners to toughen up and deal with adversity. As long as the student knows and agrees with this, and the instructor is always aware of danger signs, the benefits can be great. But abuse and corporal punishment are another story.

Because they derive from combat techniques, it can be difficult to determine the line between abuse and education. It becomes an issue of the skills and morality of the teacher, and intent. The ideal is to encourage students to push themselves to the max and offer a helping hand when needed, like a spotter at a weight training gym. There are instructors who blindly apply excessive force because they do not know any better, or who get sadistic satisfaction from making their charges suffer. This completely flies in the face of the budo spirit.

The challenge for budo instructors in Japan, one at which more than a few are struggling with, is to understand the essence of budo traditions and be inventive in how they convey to future generations. This is where a growing number of forward-thinking Japanese teachers are starting to look to the West to find ways to keep the budo spirit relevant to Japan.

A budo instructor's job is to lead by example and endure the training along with the students. This is another difference between budo and other sports. The instructor subjects himself to the same rigorous training, serving as a testing board for a constant barrage of attacks. The student sprints feverishly over short distances many times, while the teacher paces himself to run a marathon over the entire training session.

It is hard for both sides, as the teacher sacrifices his own body so that the student can increase his skill. Teacher and student are walking the same path, but if it reaches the point where the senior practitioner cannot control his emotions, then the line has been crossed and the realm of abuse has been entered. Instructors must keep a close eye on their charge's limits and abilities. This requires special expertise, vigilance, and a great deal of empathy.

In December 2012, the media reported that the captain of the basketball team at Sakuranomiya High School in Osaka killed himself after repeatedly being slapped in the face by his coach. It was the result of bullying by the teacher, and as physical as the sport is, under no circumstance is punching or slapping acceptable in basketball. Budo, however, is all about punching and slapping. It is mock combat, after all. Therefore, there is an actual danger that someone could die on the practice floor, so budo training requires an extra measure of caution compared to other sports.

It is easy for instructors of budo and sports in Japan to wander off the path of acceptable behavior and unwittingly slip into a regime of abuse. One key reason for this is the hierarchical structure of the organizations that manage sports in Japan. Japanese people are keenly aware of differences in age and rank. Being even one year older makes one a *senpai*, which means the junior *kohai* is socially obligated to obey and comply. This is characteristic of personal interaction in the dojo, sports clubs, and companies.

Sociologists describe Japan as a "vertical" society, as opposed to more egalitarian horizontal societies typical in the West. The vertical hierarchy is never more obvious than in a dojo. Even in the West, this Japanese-style pecking order is eagerly adopted in dojos, but not so much outside training. The dojo hierarchy is necessary as a safety measure to ensure that discipline is maintained at all times. Order prevents injury in the frenetic exchanges that typify a budo session.

Nevertheless, in recent years, I have noticed that young Japanese are giving less heed to rigid hierarchical relations and expectations of absolute obedience. Moreover, instructors seem less confident in their teaching and are engaging less. This is just speculation on my part, but I suspect that a gradual crumbling of the vertical hierarchies in sports and budo in Japan started when the words *risutora* (restructuring = firing superfluous staff) and *sekuhara* (sexual harassment) became common after the crash of the bubble economy in the early 1990s. Specifically, the post-bubble generations seem considerably less trusting of seniority. At least, they realize now that believing in the system brings no guarantees in life.

The traditional bonds of trust that those lower on the ladder placed in their elders has been whittled away, but the hierarchy system itself still remains. This means that the instructor may end up pandering to the students, instead of leading by example or, conversely, going overboard in trying to assert his authority. Either approach is fraught with danger. Sadly, this has seriously detracted from budo's perceived value as an educational vehicle by the wider community.

Pros and Cons of Compulsory Budo Education

Budo was a compulsory subject during World War II and was temporarily banned by Supreme Commander for the Allied Powers (SCAP) and government decree after Japan's defeat in 1945. Because it was used by the militarist regime to instil nationalist fervor, budo was viewed with suspicion and deemed too dangerous for children to learn. In the late 1950s, budo was reintroduced to the curriculum as an "optional subject" in physical education classes and extracurricular club activities.

The "National Curriculum for Middle Schools" revised in 1998 stated that the goal of budo education is not simply to drive results in terms of wins and losses as with other sports. "What is important is for pupils to gain an understanding of traditional budo ideals, to seek personal growth through training in budo technique, and develop a respectful attitude." The emphasis here is on "personal growth."

In 2012, budo was made a "compulsory subject" in all of Japan's junior high schools. What prompted the government to take this measure? A 2008 report by the Central Council for Education stated, "It is important that more instruction in budo be promoted in schools so that pupils have more hands-on contact with the unique traditions and culture of Japan." In other words, the government believes that Japanese youth need a better appreciation of their own traditional culture to function more effectively in today's global society.

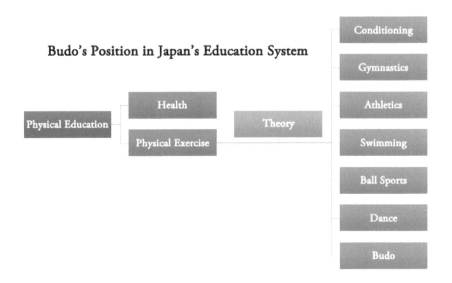

The establishment of budo as a compulsory subject was a wonderful opportunity for introducing hundreds of thousands of children to the various disciplines. One might think that, as a budo fanatic myself, I would have welcomed such a development. Instead, I have serious misgivings. Japan has over 10,000 junior high schools but no more than a few hundred teachers are truly qualified to teach budo. Principals are compelled to delegate the responsibility for budo classes at their schools to math or social studies teachers, or anybody who has studied a martial art in the past. "Hey, Tanaka, you did judo at high school, right? You've got *shodan*? Perfect!" Of course, common sense would tell you that this is far from adequate, but it is an all-too-common predicament at many schools.

Teaching budo in a slipshod fashion is perilous. Lacking experience, instructors may not know their own strength, do not recognize the inherent dangers of budo, and tend to overcompensate for their shortcomings by acting tough. Judo has been particularly tarnished by serious injuries and deaths of young practitioners over the years because of this.

Budo is battle, and hazards go with the territory. Making budo a compulsory subject in school means that scores of instructors are ill equipped to teach safely and effectively. Fortunately, budo taught in physical education classes is not so rigorous, and the time allotted for it is short. From this perspective alone, I wonder what possible benefits can be gained by making it compulsory. That aside, although the danger remains, the extracurricular club activities require the most scrutiny. Motivated by winning, instructors may become "overly enthusiastic" and take things too far. It is a double-edged sword, in that the potential for growth is immense, but so is the potential for harm. Accountability for the consequences is something that desperately needs to be addressed in Japan.

Double-Edged Sword

Budo is undeniably in the midst of an alarming tailspin in Japan, but some conscientious people are trying to do something about it. For example, in 2001 the AJJF and the Kodokan began joint sponsorship of a "Judo Renaissance." This was a movement that aimed to redirect judo to its original ideals: the perfection of the self for the benefit of society. Various federations are putting increased resources into teacher training to ensure safety at the country's schools and dojos. Changes for the better are afoot, but considerable disorientation remains.

Some of my colleagues bemoan the fact that resources are still being pumped into promoting budo internationally even though that money would be better spent domestically. Ironically, it may well be the internationalization of budo that saves it in Japan. Budo has crossed the oceans and successfully transcended cultural boundaries in countries and regions throughout the world. As I have argued, budo has a universal quality, an essence that should be preserved no matter what. The style of budo, however, needs to be flexible enough to adapt to different epochs and locations. There is nothing wrong with creating new traditions to this end, so long as the spirit, whatever that is, remains constant.

Although Japanese aficionados are happy that budo is admired outside Japan, the migration and inevitable transformation of budo as it takes root elsewhere is seen as a degradation of traditional Japanese culture. Such cultural friction is important, however, because it forces people to question their own ideals. Partly because of this, some in Japan are finally starting to realize that an unreasonable preoccupation with "traditions" that are no longer relevant is not benefitting anybody. Obsolete traditions (e.g., training methodology etc.) hinder progress. People are blinded by misconceptions that budo's core is reliant on fossilized mores that few know how to explain anymore.

The spread of budo throughout the world is a double-edged sword. This is the sword of self-surgery, cutting through the egotistical façade to unleash hidden aspects of your innermost being. This is how we grow as human beings. The global dissemination of budo has created an unexpected opportunity for Japan to reexamine what are the most salient aspects of this culture. What is it that must be treasured and passed on as accumulated wisdom to succeeding generations? What should budo be now?

Afterword

I have spent over half of my life in Japan. From time to time, I think of myself as "Alex in Wonderland," as many things here still confuse me. Still, life here is both stimulating and satisfying. When I first came in 1987, never in my wildest dreams did I think I would leave New Zealand permanently. I have now been researching budo and traditional Japanese culture intently for three decades. I fell in love with kendo, and it changed my life.

It has become my "barometer" for living. It has given me a philosophical framework to grow as a person, and its many challenges and has revealed to me my weaknesses and areas where I need to improve. No one knows what tomorrow will hold, but I do know that budo will be a part of my life to the very end.

When I tell Japanese people that I study budo, I always get the same reaction. "That's fantastic!" "You are more Japanese than I am!" "You understand the Japanese spirit, then!" If I ask them, "Ok then, what do you mean by Japanese spirit?" the standard response is "Why, Bushido, of course." "What is Bushido then?" This is where the conversation ends. Why do Japanese people have this image of budo and Bushido when more people study it outside Japan than in? This has been an important theme in my ongoing journey.

In 2008, the Japanese Budo Association published a revised version of the "Budo Charter." I was asked to translate the official version into English. It states:

> Budo, the martial ways of Japan, have their origins in the traditions of Bushido—the way of the warrior. … Practitioners study the skills while striving to unify mind, technique and body; develop his or her character; enhance their sense of morality; and to cultivate a respectful and courteous demeanor. Practiced steadfastly, these admirable traits become intrinsic to the character of the practitioner. The budo arts serve as a path to self-perfection. This elevation of the human spirit will contribute to social prosperity and harmony, and ultimately, benefit the people of the world.

Anyone reading this would think budo is a fine, upstanding form of traditional culture and something to be immensely proud of. Having watched and participated in the budo world for many years, I feel that the gap between ideals and reality has expanded, and anybody who buys into it blindly is living in a fantasy land.

The budo world should be awe inspiring, but, instead, it is plagued by political struggles among bickering factions, an overabundance of yes men in high places, bribery and other financial scandals, corporal punishment, physical abuse and hazing, doping scandals, and generally reprehensible behavior generally stemming from the priority placed on winning over everything else. The conclusion that budo has strayed far from its ideals is inescapable.

Budo authorities stress lofty ideals, but their behavior is another matter. Is this what is meant by the "Japanese spirit"? It is incumbent on budo administrators to find the proper balance between the disparate but important elements of "education" vs. "competition." It is not just the federations that bear this responsibility. Lately I have become keenly aware that we the practitioners must also share this burden.

For better or worse, I have found myself in the position of serving as a kind of bridge for budo between Japan and other countries. I am involved with budo 24/7, with my classes at the university and official roles in many different organizations as they seek to "spread the word." I often find myself at odds with attitudes of cultural imperialism driving the international dissemination of budo. But there is so much good in budo, so much beauty that glistens like diamonds in the dross, that I feel compelled to keep going.

It is often taught in budo that one should return to "the mind of the novice" (*shoshin*) to ensure your techniques and understanding of the discipline remain grounded in the fundamentals. This is achieved through humility and self-reflection, and is necessary to ensure the continued integrity of one's journey. Budo in Japan is in desperate need of a dose of its own professed medicine. As the birthplace of budo culture, Japan has a monumental responsibility to walk the talk, not just talk the talk. Some will accuse me of "preaching" in areas way beyond my station. As a "New Zealand-born Japanese," I feel an ingenuous imperative to speak candidly of my observations, and where I think budo should be right now. The fact that this book was selected by a government-appointed panel to be translated from its original Japanese into English suggests that my message was on the money and has been noticed in Japan. It is my fervent wish that this book in some way continues to contribute to a broader understanding of this wonderful thing called budo.

6 MARCH 2017

Bibliography

Bennett, Alexander. *Budo: The Martial Ways Japan.* (Tokyo: Nippon Budokan), 2009.
———. *Bushi no etosu to sono ayumi: Bushido no shakai shiso-shi teki kosatsu.* (Kyoto: Shibunkaku Co., Ltd.), 2008.
———. *Hagakure: The Secret Wisdom of the Samurai.* (VT: Tuttle), 2014.
———. *Kendo: Culture of the Sword.* (Berkeley: University of California Press), 2015.
———. *The History and Spirit of Budo.* (Chiba: IBU Budo and Sports Science Research Institute), 2010.
———. *Kano Jigoro and the Kodokan: An Innovative Response to Modernisation.* (Tokyo: Kodokan Foundation), 2009.
———. *Kendo: Culture of the Sword.* (Berkeley: University of California Press), 2015.
Chamberlain, B. H. *The Invention of a New Religion.* (London: Watts), 1912.
Daidoji Yuzan. *Budo shoshinshu.* (Tokyo: Nippon Kyoiku Bunko), 1911.
Fujiwara Masahiko. *Kokka no hinkaku.* (Tokyo: Shinchosha), 2005.
Furukawa Tetsushi. *Bushido no shiso to sono shuhen.* (Tokyo: Fukumura Shuppan Inc.), 1957.
Hobsbawm, E. Ranger, T. (eds.), *The Invention of Tradition.* (Cambridge: Cambridge University Press), 1984.
Imamura Yoshio et al. (ed.). *Budo Kasen-shu,* vols. 1 and 2. (Tokyo: Daiichi

Shobo Co., Ltd.), 1989.

———. *Nihon budo taikei,* vols. 1-2. (Kyoto: Dohosha Printing), 1982.

Inoue Tetsujiro (ed.). *Bushido zensho,* vols. 1-12. (Tokyo: Kokusho Kankokai), 1998.

Inoue Tetsujiro and Sukemasa Arima (ed.). *Bushido sosho*, vols. 1-3. (Tokyo: Hakubunkan Publishers, Ltd.), 1905.

Isogai Masayoshi and Hattori Harunori (ed.). *Koyo-gunkan,* 3 vols. (*Sengoku shiryo sosho,* vols. 3-5). (Tokyo: Jinbutsu Oraisha), 1965, 1966.

Kanno Kakumyo. *Bushido no gyakushu.* (Tokyo: Kodansha Ltd.), 2004.

Kato Jun'ichi. *Heiho-kadensho ni manabu.* (Tokyo: Nippon Budokan), 2003.

Nakabayashi Shinji. *Budo no susume.* (Tokyo: Shimazu Shobo), 1994.

Nitobe Inazo, *Bushido,* trans. Tokuhei Suchi. (Tokyo: Kodansha International), 1998.

———. *Bushido: The Soul of Japan.* (Burbank: Ohara Publications), 1979.

Sagara Toru (ed.). *Bushi no rinri: kinsei kara kindai e.* (Tokyo: Perikansha Publishing Inc.), 1993.

———. *Koyo-gunkan, Gorin-no-sho, Hagakure* (*Nihon no shiso,* vol. 9). (Tokyo: Chikuma Shobo Ltd.), 1969.

———. *Mikawa Monogatari, Hagakure* (*Nihon shiso taikei 26*). (Tokyo: Iwanami Shoten Publishers), 1974.

Sakai Kenji (ed.). *Koyo-gunkan taisei,* vols. 1-4. (Tokyo: Kyuko Shoin), 1994–95.

Sasamori Junzo. *Itto-ryu gokui.* (Tokyo: Taiiku to Sports Shuppansha), 1986.

Tahara Shiro and Morimoto Junichiro (ed.). *Yamaga Soko* (*Nihon shiso taikei 32*). (Tokyo: Iwanami Shoten Publishers), 1970.

Takano Sasaburo. *Kendo.* (Tokyo: Kendo Hakkosho), 1915.

Tominaga Kengo. *Kendo: 500 nen-shi.* (Tokyo: Hyakusen Shobo), 1971.

Uozumi Takashi (ed.). *Kaitei-ban Gorin-no-sho.* (Tokyo: Shin Jinbutsu Oraisha), 2005.

Watsuji Tetsuro. *Nihon rinri shisoshi,* vols. 1-2. (Tokyo: Iwanami Shoten Publishers), 1952.

Yasuhiko Kakei. *Chusei buke kakun no kenkyu.* (Tokyo: Kazama Shobo), 1967.
Yoshida Yutaka (trans. and ed.). *Koyo-gunkan.* (Tokyo: Tokuma Shoten), 1987.
Yuasa Akira. *Budo densho o yomu.* (Tokyo: Nippon Budokan), 2001.

ABOUT THE AUTHOR

Alexander Bennett
Alex Bennett was born in Christchurch, New Zealand, in 1970. After spending a year in at a Japanese high school as part of an exchange program and then traveling throughout Japan to study the martial arts, Bennett returned to New Zealand and attended the University of Canterbury, from which he graduated in 1994. Returning to Japan for graduate work, he received a PhD from Kyoto University (Doctor of Human and Environmental Studies) in 2001 and a second PhD from the University of Canterbury (Doctor of Philosophy in Japanese) in 2012. He has worked at the International Research Center for Japanese Studies and the Department of Japanese Studies at Teikyo University and is currently a professor in the Division of International Affairs at Kansai University. Bennett is vice president of the International Naginata Federation, a member of the International Committee of the All Japan Kendo Federation, International Committee of the All Japan Jukendo Federation, a director of the Japanese Academy of Budo, and a head coach with NZ Kendo. Bennett founded and serves as editor-in-chief of Kendo World, the world's only English-language journal dedicated to kendo, and holds the grades of kendo *kyoshi* 7-*dan*, *iaido* 5-*dan*, *naginata* 5-*dan*, *tankendo* 5-*dan*, *jukendo* 5-*dan*, and Jikishinkage-ryu *kenjutsu* 3-*dan*. He also studies Tendo-ryu *naginata-jutsu*. He has competed successfully at international competitions in *naginata* and kendo, taking second place at the World Naginata Championships in July 2011 and leading the New Zealand National Kendo Team to the top eight at the fifteenth World Kendo Championship. Bennett is also a prolific writer in both Japanese and English on Japanese history and culture. Recent publications in English include *Hagakure: The Secret Wisdom of the Samurai* (Tuttle, 2014), *Kendo: Culture of the Sword* (University of California Press, 2015), and *Naginata: History and Practice* (Bunkasha International, 2016).

（英文版）日本人の知らない武士道
Bushido and the Art of Living: An Inquiry into Samurai Values

2019年2月28日　第1刷発行

著者　　　アレキサンダー・ベネット
発行所　　一般財団法人出版文化産業振興財団
　　　　　〒101-0051 東京都千代田区神田神保町3-12-3
　　　　　電話　03-5211-7282（代）
　　　　　ホームページ　http://www.jpic.or.jp/japanlibrary/

印刷・製本所　株式会社ウイル・コーポレーション

定価はカバーに表示してあります。
本書の無断複写（コピー）、転載は著作権法
の例外を除き、禁じられています。

© 2013 by Alexander Bennett
Printed in Japan
ISBN 978-4-86658-051-7